大学英语立体化网络化系列教材　　李淑静 / 总主编

Boya
College English

博雅英语 4

（第二版）

主　编 / 张文霞
副主编 / 蔡　蔚
编　者 /（按姓氏拼音排列）
　　　　徐　溯　郑文博　周允程

图书在版编目(CIP)数据

博雅英语.4 / 李淑静总主编. -- 2版. -- 北京：北京大学出版社，2024.8.--（大学英语立体化网络化系列教材）. -- ISBN 978-7-301-35494-0

Ⅰ. H319.39

中国国家版本馆CIP数据核字第20242W3Z65号

书　　名	博雅英语(4)(第二版) BOYA YINGYU (4) (DI-ER BAN)
著作责任者	李淑静　总主编
责任编辑	李　娜
标准书号	ISBN 978-7-301-35494-0
出版发行	北京大学出版社
地　　址	北京市海淀区成府路205号　100871
网　　址	http://www.pup.cn　新浪微博:@北京大学出版社
电子邮箱	编辑部 pupwaiwen@pup.cn　总编室 zpup@pup.cn
电　　话	邮购部 010-62752015　发行部 010-62750672　编辑部 010-62754382
印刷者	北京虎彩文化传播有限公司
经销者	新华书店
	787毫米×1092毫米　16开本　9.25印张　380千字 2015年11月第1版　2024年8月第2版　2024年8月第1次印刷
定　　价	58.00元

未经许可，不得以任何方式复制或抄袭本书之部分或全部内容。
版权所有，侵权必究
举报电话：010-62752024　电子邮箱：fd@pup.cn
图书如有印装质量问题，请与出版部联系，电话：010-62756370

前 言

古希腊、古罗马倡导的博雅教育（Liberal Education），旨在传授广博的知识，培养独立完善的人格和优雅的气质，使人不仅获得专业技能，而且陶冶品学才识，成为完全的人。与之相辉映，中华文化传统如《论语》之"子曰：君子不器"，以及《大学》之"大学之道，在明明德，在亲民，在止于至善"，也强调人应该有完善的人格，不能像器具一样，只满足某一种用途。

北京大学教材建设委员会设立的大学英语教材改革项目《博雅英语》，正是要达到这样的目的，将大学英语课程的工具性和人文性有机统一，使之作为高等学校人文教育的一部分，体现高等教育区别于基础教育的特点，以教材的思想性带动语言学习，不仅增强学生的英语综合应用能力和自主学习能力，而且发展学生的跨文化交际能力和批判性思维能力。

人文性目标首先体现在对教学材料的选择上。《博雅英语》通过走访人文社科领域学者和调研学习者需求，在选材上确定了"语言与文学、历史与文明、哲学与人生、建筑与艺术、法制与民主、经济与社会、人与自然、科技与教育"等八个主题板块。所选听读材料既有中西方经典作品或其介绍，也有对现实生活中热点问题的分析或讨论，力图达到经典与时代的结合、西方文化与中华文化的互动、人文素养与科学精神的交融，彰显教育的根本——立德树人，使学生在批判性的英语学习中，吸收优秀的文化、观念和正确的价值观，培养跨文化国际视野和中国情怀，树立文化自觉和文化自信，未来成为中外文化交流及"讲好中国故事，传播好中国声音，阐释好中国特色"的重要力量。

在教学材料的编排上，《博雅英语》遵循语言学习发展规律，力图贯彻"以输入为基础、以输出为驱动"的理念，注重经典阅读、培养思辨能力、强化书面及口头表达能力。每个主题单元都由四个板块构成：视听导入（Lead-in）、从读到写（Reading and Writing）、从读到说（Reading and Speaking）、跨文化交流（Cross Cultural Communication），以听读促写、以听读促说、以英汉互译促跨文化学习及中国文化传播，融合听、说、读、写、译各种语言技能，促进学生综合语言应用能力的养成。在学习活动的设计中，《博雅英语》尤其注重开放性，启发学生对经典的感受能力，培养批判性思维习惯，引导学生主动学习、自主学习和个性化地学习，培养发现问题、分析问题、解决问题的创新能力。

《博雅英语》力求构建优质的教学资源共享体系，发挥好教材在引导教师转变教学观念、调整教学方式等方面的功能和作用。在提供学生用书、教师用书及相应的电子资源的同时，还将组织授课教师围绕教材的重点、难点、疑点或某些教学环节开发微课，以视频为主要载体记录并分享其教育教学活动的精彩内容，并通过开放性的网络平台鼓励师生共同构建教学资源，交流学习成果，营造出一个个真实的微教学资源环境和学习共同体。

在大学英语课程改革不断深化的新阶段，全体编者期望通过编写《博雅英语》，为丰富大学英语课程的人文内涵、实现其工具性与人文性的有机统一、促进学生的综合素质提高和全面发展尽自己的绵薄之力。不足之处难免，敬请批评指正。

李淑静

2022年12月

Contents

Unit 1 LANGUAGE AND LITERATURE ···1
    Part One   Lead-in ··2
                         Section 1   Listening   The Chinese Language ···················2
                         Section 2   Watching   The Hours ·······························2
    Part Two   Reading and Writing ··2
                         Text A   The Mark on the Wall ·······························3
    Part Three   Reading and Speaking ···8
                         Text B   In Theory: the Death of Literature ···············8
    Part Four   Cross Cultural Communication ····································13
                         Passage A   甲骨文的发现 ·······································13
                         Passage B   Formal and Substantive Universals of
                                             Languages ································14

Unit 2 HISTORY AND CIVILIZATION ···17
    Part One   Lead-in ··18
                         Section 1   Listening   Cultural Diversity and Assimilation in
                                         America: a Failure? ·····························18
                         Section 2   Watching   Ancient Egypt ··························18
    Part Two   Reading and Writing ··18
                         Text A   On History ···19
    Part Three   Reading and Speaking ···25
                         Text B   Chinese and Western Civilization Contrasted ···········25
    Part Four   Cross Cultural Communication ····································29
                         Passage A   丝绸之路与文化交流 ··························29
                         Passage B   The Process of Civilisation ······················31

Unit 3 PHILOSOPHY AND LIFE ···33
    Part One   Lead-in ··34
                         Section 1   Listening   Problems of Philosophy ············34
                         Section 2   Watching   Zeno Paradox ··························34
    Part Two   Reading and Writing ··34
                         Text A   What Philosophy Is For ····························35

	Part Three	Reading and Speaking ··· 41
		Text B Meaning in Life ································· 41
	Part Four	Cross Cultural Communication ······························ 45
		Passage A 中国哲学的线索 ···························· 45
		Passage B What Is Enlightenment? ···················· 46

Unit 4 MUSIC AND THE SOCIAL WORLD ································ 50

	Part One	Lead-in ··· 51
		Section 1 Listening Preference for Familiar or Unfamiliar Sounds? ························ 51
		Section 2 Watching Arches in Music and Architecture ········ 51
	Part Two	Reading and Writing ······································ 52
		Text A Why Premieres? ···························· 52
	Part Three	Reading and Speaking ···································· 59
		Text B Music and the Social World ················ 59
	Part Four	Cross Cultural Communication ···························· 63
		Passage A 中国古代音乐的文化内涵 ··············· 63
		Passage B The Musical Legacies of Antiquity ········ 64

Unit 5 DEMOCRACY AND LAW ·· 68

	Part One	Lead-in ··· 69
		Section 1 Listening Rawls and His Theory of Justice ········ 69
		Section 2 Watching Introduction to Political Philosophy ······ 69
	Part Two	Reading and Writing ······································ 70
		Text A Two Principles of Justice ················· 70
	Part Three	Reading and Speaking ···································· 76
		Text B Equality, Liberty and Democracy ·········· 77
	Part Four	Cross Cultural Communication ···························· 81
		Passage A "仁"和"礼" ································ 81
		Passage B On Liberty ································ 82

Unit 6 ECONOMY AND SOCIETY ·· 86

	Part One	Lead-in ··· 87
		Section 1 Listening Why Should We Study Past Economic Thinkers ···················· 87
		Section 2 Watching A Beautiful Mind: The Nash Equilibrium ························ 87

Contents

	Part Two	Reading and Writing	87
		Text A Individuals in Foreign Trade	88
	Part Three	Reading and Speaking	93
		Text B How Did Economists Get It So Wrong?	94
	Part Four	Cross Cultural Communication	99
		Passage A 孙子兵法	99
		Passage B The Merchant of Venice	101

Unit 7 NATURE AND HUMAN SOCIETY ... 108

- Part One　　Lead-in ... 109
  - Section 1　Listening　English Lake District: Landscape and the Wild ... 109
  - Section 2　Watching　Beethoven and His Pastoral Symphony ... 109
- Part Two　　Reading and Writing ... 109
  - Text A　Preface to *Animal Liberation* ... 110
- Part Three　Reading and Speaking ... 116
  - Text B　We Have No Duty to Animals ... 116
- Part Four　Cross Cultural Communication ... 119
  - Passage A　醉翁亭记 ... 119
  - Passage B　Lines Composed a Few Miles Above Tintern Abbey, on Revisiting the Banks of the Wye During a Tour ... 120

Unit 8 TECHNOLOGY AND ETHICS ... 125

- Part One　　Lead-in ... 126
  - Section 1　Listening　Epidemic Disease: Is the Internet Our Key to Survival? ... 126
  - Section 2　Watching　The Truman Show: The Interview ... 126
- Part Two　　Reading and Writing ... 127
  - Text A　Has Big Data Made Anonymity Impossible? ... 127
- Part Three　Reading and Speaking ... 132
  - Text B　From Privacy to Accountability ... 133
- Part Four　Cross Cultural Communication ... 137
  - Passage A　《劝学篇》序 ... 137
  - Passage B　Precursors of Modern Science ... 138

Unit 1

LANGUAGE AND LITERATURE

Shot out at the feet of God entirely naked! Tumbling head over heels in the asphodel meadows like brown paper parcels pitched down a shoot in the post office! With one's hair flying back like the tail of a race-horse. Yes, that seems to express the rapidity of life, the perpetual waste and repair; all so casual, all so haphazard....

—*Virginia Woolf*

Learning Objectives

Upon the completion of this unit, you should be able to:

Remembering & Understanding	★ master the spelling and usages of new words and phrases of text A and text B; ★ read text A and text B with full knowledge of their intended meaning;
Analyzing & Applying	★ make reference to the techniques and/or main ideas of text A and text B in your writing and discussion; ★ express complex ideas and emotions on the subjects of language and literature in oral and written forms;
Evaluating & Creating	★ agree or disagree with others' opinions and ideas on language and literature; ★ reproduce texts in your own language to display the ability of cross-cultural communication; ★ present the life and works of a female Chinese writer.

Part One Lead-in

Section 1 Listening

Directions: Please fill in the blanks with words or sentences on the basis of what you have heard in the audio clip. Then discuss the following questions in pairs or groups.

The Chinese Language

Every nation has developed a writing 1 _____ to its language. Europe did not develop a writing on pictorial principle because the phonetic structure of Indo-Germanic words, with its comparative profusion of consonants and infinitely variable combinations, required an analytic alphabet, and would make the representation of these words by pictographs 2 _____. For no system of ideographs could be used alone, and it was found, as in the case of Chinese, 3 _____ the pictorial principle by the phonetic principle before it could have any important development. These elementary pictographs were then 4 _____ purely for their phonetic value, and actually nine-tenths of the over forty thousand characters in Chinese dictionaries are built on 5 _____, with about thirteen hundred ideographs as phonetic signs.

6. Could you give two or three characteristics that you think are unique to the Chinese language?
7. What special relationship does the Chinese language have with Chinese literature and thought? Why didn't Europe develop a writing on pictorial principle?
8. How did every nation develop a writing most suitable to its language?
9. Do you generally agree with the speaker's observations about the Chinese language? Please give your reasons.

Section 2 Watching

Directions: Please watch the video clip and discuss the following questions in pairs or groups.

The Hours

1. Who do you think the woman in the film might be speaking to? What exactly does she say to him/her?
2. What is the woman trying to do? What is the main reason she gives for doing it?
3. Can you describe the feelings and emotions evoked from watching the film clip? Given the choice, would you like to watch the complete film? Give your reasons.

Part Two Reading and Writing

Pre-Reading Questions

1. What can you say about a mark on the wall?
2. Do you often wonder about the significance of small and seemingly unimportant objects or beings in the world? What are they? What are your thoughts on them?

Unit 1

Text A

The Mark on the Wall
(*Excerpt*)
Virginia Woolf

1   Perhaps it was the middle of January in the present year that I first looked up and saw the mark on the wall. In order to fix a date it is necessary to remember what one saw. So now I think of the fire; the steady film of yellow light upon the page of my book; the three *chrysanthemums* in the round glass bowl on the mantelpiece. Yes, it must have been the winter time, and we had just finished our tea, for I remember that I was smoking a cigarette when I looked up and saw the mark on the wall for the first time. I looked up through the smoke of my cigarette and my eye lodged for a moment upon the burning coals, and that old fancy of the crimson flag flapping from the castle tower came into my mind, and I thought of the cavalcade of red knights riding up the side of the black rock. Rather to my relief the sight of the mark interrupted the fancy, for it is an old fancy, an automatic fancy, made as a child perhaps. The mark was a small round mark, black upon the white wall, about six or seven inches above the mantelpiece.

2   How readily our thoughts swarm upon a new object, lifting it a little way, as ants carry a blade of straw so feverishly, and then leave it.... If that mark was made by a nail, it can't have been for a picture, it must have been for a *miniature*—the miniature of a lady with white powdered curls, powder-dusted cheeks, and lips like red *carnations*. A fraud of course, for the people who had this house before us would have chosen pictures in that way—an old picture for an old room. That is the sort of people they were—very interesting people, and I think of them so often, in such queer places, because one will never see them again, never know what happened next. They wanted to leave this house because they wanted to change their style of furniture, so he said, and he was in process of saying that in his opinion art should have ideas behind it when we were torn asunder, as one is torn from the old lady about to pour out tea and the young man about to hit the tennis ball in the back garden of the suburban villa as one rushes past in the train.

3   But as for that mark, I'm not sure about it; I don't believe it was made by a nail after all; it's too big, too round, for that. I might get up, but if I got up and looked at it, ten to one I shouldn't be able to say *for certain*; because once a thing's done, no one ever knows how it happened. Oh! *dear me*, the mystery of life; The inaccuracy of thought! The ignorance of humanity! To show how very little control of our possessions we have—what an accidental affair this living is after all our civilization—let me just count over a few of the things lost in one lifetime, beginning, for that seems always the most mysterious of losses—what cat would gnaw, what rat would nibble—three pale blue canisters of book-binding tools? Then there were the bird cages, the iron hoops,

the steel skates, the Queen Anne coal-scuttle, the bagatelle board, the *hand organ*—all gone, and jewels, too. *Opals* and *emeralds*, they *lie about* the roots of *turnips*. What a scraping paring affair it is to be sure! The wonder is that I've any clothes on my back, that I sit surrounded by solid furniture at this moment. Why, if one wants to compare life to anything, one must liken it to being blown through the Tube at fifty miles an hour—landing at the other end without a single hairpin in one's hair! Shot out at the feet of God entirely naked! Tumbling *head over heels* in the *asphodel* meadows like brown paper parcels pitched down a shoot in the post office! With one's hair flying back like the tail of a race-horse. Yes, that seems to express the rapidity of life, the *perpetual* waste and repair; all so casual, all so *haphazard*....

4   But after life. The slow pulling down of thick green *stalks* so that the cup of the flower, as it turns over, deluges one with purple and red light. Why, after all, should one not be born there as one is born here, helpless, speechless, unable to focus one's eyesight, groping at the roots of the grass, at the toes of the Giants? As for saying which are trees, and which are men and women, or whether there are such things, that one won't be in a condition to do for fifty years or so. There will be nothing but spaces of light and dark, intersected by thick stalks, and rather higher up perhaps, rose-shaped blots of an indistinct colour—dim pinks and blues—which will, as time goes on, become more definite, become—I don't know what....

5   And yet that mark on the wall is not a hole at all. It may even be caused by some round black substance, such as a small rose leaf, left over from the summer, and I, not being a very *vigilant* housekeeper—look at the dust on the mantelpiece, for example, the dust which, so they say, buried Troy three times over, only fragments of pots utterly refusing *annihilation,* as one can believe.

6   The tree outside the window taps very gently on the pane.... I want to think quietly, calmly, spaciously, never to be interrupted, never to have to rise from my chair, to slip easily from one thing to another, without any sense of hostility, or *obstacle*. I want to sink deeper and deeper, away from the surface, with its hard separate facts. To steady myself, let me *catch hold of* the first idea that passes.... Shakespeare.... Well, he will do as well as another. A man who sat himself solidly in an arm-chair, and looked into the fire, so—A shower of ideas fell perpetually from some very high Heaven down through his mind. He leant his forehead on his hand, and people, looking in through the open door,—for this scene is supposed to take place on a summer's evening—But how dull this is, this historical fiction! It doesn't interest me at all. I wish I could hit upon a pleasant track of thought, a track indirectly reflecting credit upon myself, for those are the pleasantest thoughts, and very frequent even in the minds of modest mouse-coloured people, who believe genuinely that they dislike to hear their own praises. They are not thoughts directly praising oneself; that is the beauty of them...

(1181 words)

Unit 1

New Words

chrysanthemum	[krɪˈsænθəməm]	*n.*	a garden plant with large brightly coloured flowers 菊花
miniature	[ˈmɪnɪtʃə]	*n.*	exactly like something or someone but much smaller 缩图；微型画；微型图画绘画术
carnation	[kɑːˈneɪʃ(ə)n]	*n.*	a sweet-smelling white, pink, or red flower 康乃馨
opal	[ˈəʊp(ə)l]	*n.*	a precious stone which looks like milky water with colours in it 猫眼石，蛋白石；乳白玻璃
emerald	[ˈem(ə)r(ə)ld]	*n.*	a bright green precious stone 绿宝石；[宝] 祖母绿
turnip	[ˈtɜːnɪp]	*n.*	a round vegetable which grows underground and is used as food 萝卜；芜菁甘蓝，大头菜
asphodel	[ˈæsfədel]	*n.*	any of various chiefly Mediterranean plants of the genera Asphodeline and Asphodelus having linear leaves and racemes of white or pink or yellow flowers 水仙；日光兰；常春花
perpetual	[pəˈpetʃuəl]	*adj.*	continuing all the time without changing or stopping 永久的；不断的；无期限的
haphazard	[hæpˈhæzəd]	*adj.*	dependent upon or characterized by chance 偶然的；随便的；无计划的
stalk	[stɔːk]	*n.*	a long narrow part of a plant that supports leaves, fruits, or flowers（植物的）茎，秆；（支持叶子、果实和花的）梗，柄
vigilant	[ˈvɪdʒɪl(ə)nt]	*adj.*	giving careful attention to what is happening, so that you will notice any danger or illegal activity 警惕的；警醒的；注意的；警戒的
annihilation	[ənaɪɪˈleɪʃ(ə)n]	*n.*	total destruction 灭绝；消灭
obstacle	[ˈɒbstək(ə)l]	*n.*	something that makes it difficult to achieve something 障碍，干扰；妨害物

New Expressions

for certain	definitely or positively 确定
dear me	You say "dear me" when you are sad, disappointed, or surprised about something（表示悲伤、失望、惊讶等）啊呀；哎唷
hand organ	a large machine that plays music when you turn the handle on the side. Barrel organs used to be played in the street to entertain people 手摇风琴
lie about	hang around idly 无所事事
head over heels	in disorderly haste 颠倒地；头朝下

catch hold of   to take hold of or grab something 抓牢；抓住

Notes

Virginia Woolf (25 January 1882—28 March 1941) was an English writer and one of the foremost modernists of the twentieth century. During the interwar period, Woolf was a significant figure in London literary society and a central figure in the influential Bloomsbury Group of intellectuals. Her most famous works include the novels *Mrs Dalloway* (1925), *To the Lighthouse* (1927) and *Orlando: A Biography* (1928), and the book-length essay *A Room of One's Own* (1929), with its famous dictum, "A woman must have money and a room of her own if she is to write fiction." Woolf suffered from severe bouts of mental illness throughout her life, thought to have been the result of what is now termed bipolar disorder, and committed suicide by drowning in 1941 at the age of 59. The text is excerpted from her essay *The Mark on the Wall*.

Task 1   Generating the Outline

Directions: Please identify the thesis of the passage and the main point of each paragraph, and then find out how these points develop the thesis.

_____
_____
_____
_____
_____
_____
_____

Task 2   Understanding the Text

Directions: Please answer the following questions based on Text A.

1. How does the author gradually build up her narrative about the mark on the wall?
2. How does the author manage to lead the reader into thinking beyond the mark on the wall?
3. Compared with other stories you have read, what is unusual about this one? Does it have a clear plot? How does the story make sense to you?
4. What are the possible causes given by the author that might have resulted in the mark on the wall?
5. What is the author trying to say about life when she claims "if one wants to compare life to anything, one must liken it to being blown through the Tube at fifty miles an hour"?
6. The narrator's mind drifts between the identity of the mark on the wall and the meaning of life. Is there a relationship between the two that the narrator is implying?
7. How far do you agree or disagree with the narrator's opinions about the meaning of life? What is the meaning of life to you?

Unit 1

Task 3 Learning the Words and Phrases

Directions: Please fill in the blanks in the sentences below with the words or phrases listed in the box. Change the forms if necessary.

> vigilant   perpetual   head over heels   stealthily

1. But how do you keep from choosing a dubious financial partner while falling _____?
2. Using solar power, "we are close to the notion of _____ flight," he said.
3. In terms of self-protection, the Home Office advises the public to be above all _____.
4. Sir Percy usually made his points, and got his way, _____ and quietly.

Task 4 Translating the Sentences

Directions: Please translate the following sentences into Chinese.

1. So now I think of the fire; the steady film of yellow light upon the page of my book; the three chrysanthemums in the round glass bowl on the mantelpiece.

2. I looked up through the smoke of my cigarette and my eye lodged for a moment upon the burning coals, and that old fancy of the crimson flag flapping from the castle tower came into my mind, and I thought of the cavalcade of red knights riding up the side of the black rock.

3. Rather to my relief the sight of the mark interrupted the fancy, for it is an old fancy, an automatic fancy, made as a child perhaps.

4. How readily our thoughts swarm upon a new object, lifting it a little way, as ants carry a blade of straw so feverishly, and then leave it...

Task 5 Writing Exercises

Directions: Please answer the following questions according to your understanding of the text.

What are the special writing techniques used in this text that make it unusual? What is the central idea that the author wishes to convey?

_____
_____
_____

Directions: Write a short story or essay in English in about 300 words; try to use some of the writing techniques employed in this text if you can.

_____
_____
_____

Part Three   Reading and Speaking

Pre-Reading Questions

1. What role does literature play in your life? How frequently do you read literary works?
2. Upon reading the title, what do you predict the author is going to talk about?

Text B

In Theory: the Death of Literature
(*Excerpt*)
Andrew Gallix

1 "We come too late to say anything which has not been said already," *lamented* La Bruyère at the end of the 17th century. The fact that he came too late even to say this (Terence having pipped him to the post back in the 2nd century BC) merely proved his point—a point which Macedonio Fernández took one step backwards when he sketched out a *prequel* to Genesis. God is just about to create everything. Suddenly a voice in the wilderness *pipes up*, interrupting the *eternal* silence of infinite space that so terrified Pascal: "Everything has been written, everything has been said, everything has been done." Rolling His eyes, the Almighty retorts (doing his best Morrissey impression) that he has heard this one before—many a time. He then presses ahead with the creation of the heavens and the earth and all the creepy-crawlies that creepeth and

crawleth upon it. In the beginning was the word—and, word is, before that too.

2   In his most influential book, *The Anxiety of Influence* (1973), Harold Bloom argued that the greatest Romantic poets misread their *illustrious* predecessors "*so as to* clear imaginative space for themselves". The literary father figure was killed, figuratively speaking, through a process of "poetic misprision". T.S. Eliot had already expressed a similar idea in 1920, when he claimed that "Immature poets imitate; mature poets steal; bad poets deface what they take, and good poets make it into something better, or at least something different". Borges (a disciple of Fernández, whom Bloom references) was on the same wavelength (but at the other end of the dial) when he claimed that "each writer creates his *precursors*".

3   According to Bloom, this feeling of "secondariness" is not specifically a Romantic phenomenon, but rather the very engine of literary history. Down the centuries, literature has always been a two-way dialogue between past and present—the former living on in the latter; the latter casting new light upon the former. George Steiner thus contends that the highest form of literary criticism is to be found within literature itself: "In the poet's criticism of the poet from within the poem, *hermeneutics* reads the living text which Hermes, the messenger, has brought from the undying dead" (*Real Presences*, 1989). This implies that writing is not, primarily, about self-expression, but about reception and transmission; as Winnie the Pooh once put it, with uncharacteristic *menace*, "Poetry and Hums aren't things which you get, they're things which get you". What is striking here is that Steiner—steeped in the Judaeo-Christian tradition; scourge of Gallic theory—should be in total agreement, on this point, with novelist Tom McCarthy, who comes, as it were, from the other side of the *barricades*. For the author of *C*—a novel which is all about fiction as reception and transmission—"the writer is a receiver and the content is already out there. The task of the writer is to filter it, to sample it and remix it—not in some random way, but conscientiously and attentively." Turning *chronology* on its head, he sees *Finnegans Wake* as the source code of *anglophone* literature—a new beginning—rather than a dead end or a full stop. The novel, says McCarthy, has been "living out its own death" ever since *Don Quixote*; the "experience of failure" being integral to its DNA. If it weren't dying, the novel would not be alive.

4   According to Steiner, the rise of the novel was contemporaneous with a growing linguistic crisis. After the 17th century—after Milton—"the sphere of language" ceased to encompass most of "experience and reality" (*The Retreat from the Word*, 1961). Mathematics became increasingly untranslatable into words, post-Impressionist painting likewise escaped verbalisation; linguistics and philosophy highlighted the fact that words *refer to* other words… The final proposition in Wittgenstein's *Tractatus* (1921) *bears witness to* this *encroachment* of the unspeakable: "Whereof one cannot speak, thereof one must be silent." Four years earlier, Kafka had conjectured that it may have been possible to escape the *sirens*' singing, but not their silence.

5   Harold Bloom is right: belatedness is not merely an "historical condition". After all, it was already one of the major themes in *Don Quixote*. Yet, as Gabriel Josipovici points out, "this sense of somehow having arrived too late, of having lost for ever something that was once a common possession, is a, if not the, key Romantic concern" (*What Ever Happened to Modernism?* 2010). Against the backdrop of declining confidence in the powers of language—just as Schiller's "*disenchantment* of the world" was becoming ever more apparent, and the writer's legitimacy, in a "*destitute* time" (Hölderlin) of absent gods and silent sirens, seemed increasingly *arbitrary*—literature came to be considered as an "absolute". Walter Benjamin famously described the "birthplace of the novel" as "the *solitary* individual": an individual cut off from tradition, who could no longer claim to be the mouthpiece of society. As soon as this "solitary individual" was elevated to the status of an alter deus, the essential belatedness of human creativity became glaringly obvious. "No art form," says Steiner, "comes out of nothing. Always, it comes after, and the human maker rages at [this] coming after, at being, forever, second to the original and originating mystery of the forming of form".

6   As early as 1758, Samuel Richardson had wondered if the novel were not just a fad, whose time had already run out. By the 20th century, the picture looked far bleaker. Theodor Adorno felt that there could be no poetry after Auschwitz. In 1959, Brion Gysin complained that fiction was lagging 50 years behind painting. In the early 60s, Alain Robbe-Grillet attacked the mummification of the novel in its 19th-century incarnation. In 1967, John Barth published "The Literature of Exhaustion" in which he spoke of "the used-upness of certain forms or exhaustion of certain possibilities". The same year, Gore Vidal diagnosed that the novel was already in its death throes: "we shall go on for quite a long time talking of books and writing books, pretending all the while not to notice that the church is empty and the *parishioners* have gone elsewhere to attend other gods". The death of literature, and the world as we know it, became a fashionable topic among US academics in the early 90s (see, for instance, Alvin Kernan's aptly-titled *The Death of Literature*, 1992). Their argument was usually that English departments had been hijacked by cultural studies, Continental theory or political correctness gone mad.

(1087 words)

New Words

| lament | [ləˈment] | v. | express grief verbally, regret strongly 哀悼；悲叹；悔恨 |
| prequel | [ˈpriːkwəl] | n. | A prequel is a literary, dramatic, or filmic work whose story precedes that of a previous work, by focusing on events that occur before the original narrative; A prequel is a work that forms part of |

Unit 1

			a back-story to the preceding work. 据已问世文艺作品的情节凭想象上溯创作的前篇,先行篇,前传
eternal	[ɪˈtɜːn(ə)l]	*adj.*	continuing forever or indefinitely, tiresomely long; seemingly without end 永恒的;不朽的
illustrious	[ɪˈlʌstrɪəs]	*adj.*	widely known and esteemed, having or conferring glory 著名的,杰出的;辉煌的
precursor	[prɪˈkɜːsə]	*adj.*	a person who goes before or announces the coming of another, an indication of the approach of something or someone 先驱,前导
hermeneutics	[ˌhɜːmɪˈnjuːtɪks]	*n.*	the branch of theology that deals with principles of exegesis 解释学;诠释学
menace	[ˈmenəs]	*n.*	something that is a source of danger, a threat or the act of threatening 威胁;恐吓
barricade	[ˌbærɪˈkeɪd]	*n.*	a barrier set up by police to stop traffic on a street or road in order to catch a fugitive or inspect traffic, etc. 街垒;路障
chronology	[krəˈnɒlədʒɪ]	*adj.*	an arrangement of events in time, a record of events in the order of their occurrence 年表;年代学
anglophone	[ˈæŋglə(ʊ)fəʊn]	*n.*	people whose mother tongue is English 以英语为母语的人
encroachment	[enˈkrəʊtʃm(ə)nt]	*n.*	any entry into an area not previously occupied, influencing strongly 侵入,侵犯;侵蚀
siren	[ˈsaɪr(ə)n]	*n.*	a sea nymph (part woman and part bird) supposed to lure sailors to destruction on the rocks where the nymphs lived; a warning signal that is a loud wailing sound 汽笛;迷人的女人;歌声动人的女歌手
disenchantment	[ˌdɪs(ɪ)nˈtʃɑːntm(ə)nt]	*n.*	freeing from false belief or illusions 醒悟,清醒;不抱幻想
destitute	[ˈdestɪtjuːt]	*adj.*	completely wanting or lacking 穷困的;无;缺乏的
arbitrary	[ˈɑːbɪt(rə)rɪ]	*adj.*	based on or subject to individual discretion or preference or sometimes impulse or caprice 任意的;武断的;专制的
solitary	[ˈsɒlɪt(ə)rɪ]	*adj.*	lacking companions or companionship 孤独的;独居的
parishioner	[pəˈrɪʃ(ə)nə]	*n.*	a member of a parish 教区居民

pipe up	to commence singing or playing a musical instrument 吹奏乐曲
so as to	so that 为使，以便
refer to	involve; mention 涉及，谈到，提到；关系到
bear witness to	witness; prove; serve as witness / evidence to something 证明；作证；成为……的证人(或见证、证据)

The text is excerpted from an article published in the literary section of 10 January 2012 issue of *The Guardian*. *The Guardian* is a British national daily newspaper. Founded in 1821, it was known as *The Manchester Guardian* until 1959. From its beginnings as a local paper it has grown into a national paper associated with a complex organisational structure and an international multi-media and web presence. Its sister papers include *The Observer* (a British Sunday paper) and *The Guardian Weekly*. In August 2013 *The Guardian* in paper form had an average daily circulation of 189,000 copies, behind *The Daily Telegraph* and *The Times*, and ahead of *The Independent*.

Task 1   Questions for Comprehension

Directions: Please answer the following questions based on Text B.

1. What is the author trying to say by quoting La Bruyère at the beginning of the article?
2. What is the meaning of "poetic misprision"? How far do you agree or disagree with T.S. Eliot's opinions about different types of poets?
3. How far do you agree or disagree with George Steiner's perception about "the highest form of literary criticism"?
4. What is your understanding about literature being "a two-way dialogue between past and present"?
5. Why do you think McCarthy believes that the novel has been "living out its own death" ever since *Don Quixote*?
6. What are the general feelings about the fate of the novel in the 20th century?

Task 2   Questions for Discussion

Directions: Discuss the following questions in pairs or groups.

1. Do you think literature is dying, has been dying for a long time, or is alive and well? Give your reasons.
2. What is the position of literature in modern society? What do you think is the function of literature?
3. What are the issues touched upon by the author? What are the main arguments? How far do you agree or disagree with the author?
4 Work out a list of possible arguments that are either for or against the following statement: Literature is becoming increasingly useless in modern society.

5. Exchange and discuss your opinions with others, and make a summary of the most important arguments made by the group.

Part Four Cross Cultural Communication

Passage A

甲骨文的发现

甲骨文的发现是中国近代学术史上的一件大事。清晚期在河南省北部的安阳县,彰德府所在的县城西北五里,有村名小屯,其地处洹水之南,即历史上项羽大败秦军于漳水之南,章邯求议盟,"项羽乃与期洹水南殷虚上"(见《史记·项羽本纪》)的殷墟。当地农民多种植棉花、麦子与小米,在刨地时往往有"字骨头"出土,或用以填塞枯井,或则磨粉作刀尖药于集市中出售,或称斤卖给药材店作为药材中的龙骨和龟板。村中有李成者,剃头为业,以出售"龙骨"粉配制成的刀尖药为副业,也成批卖给当地药材店,因为龙骨不能有字,故凡有字的都事先刮去。现在已无法估计会有多少甲骨被当作药品毁掉。这是无法弥补的损失。关于这种情况,罗振常在《洹洛访古游记》宣统三年(1911)二月二十三日游记里曾记载道:"此地埋藏龟甲,前三十余年已发现,不自今日始也。谓某年某姓犁田,忽有数骨片随土翻起,视之,上有刻画,且有作殷色者(即涂朱者),不知为何物。北方土中,埋藏物多,每耕耘,或见稍奇之物,随即其处掘之,往往得铜器、古泉、古镜等,得善价……且古骨研末,又愈刀创,故药铺购之,一斤才得数钱。骨之坚者,或又购以刻物。乡人农暇,随地发掘,所得甚夥,检大者售之。购者或不取刻文,则以铲削之而售。"

光绪二十五年(1899)秋季,有山东潍县的古董商范维卿将甲骨贩卖到北京,以甲骨文十二版售与国子监祭酒王懿荣,每版价银二两(《甲骨年表》据明义士《甲骨研究》讲义引范贾所言)。翌年庚子(1900)丹徒刘鹗在《铁云藏龟·自序》中亦云:"庚子岁有范姓客挟百余片走京师,福山王文敏公懿荣见之狂喜,以厚价留之。后有潍县赵君执斋得数百片,亦售归文敏。"是年七月,八国联军侵京,王氏殉难,二十八年(1902)其子崇烈售其先父所藏古器物以清夙债,甲骨千余片尽归刘鹗。其实最早鉴定收藏甲骨的除王懿荣之外应推天津的孟定生与王襄两位穷秀才,据王襄《题易橘园殷契拓册》,刊于1935年《河北博物院半月刊》第八五期)说:"当发现之时,村农收落花生果,偶于土中检之,不知其贵也。潍贾范寿轩辈见而来收,亦不知其贵也。范贾售古器物来余斋,座上讼言所见,乡人孟定生世叔闻之,意为古简,促其诣车访求,时则清光绪戊戌(1898)冬十月也。翌年秋,携来求售,名之曰龟版。人世知有殷契自此始。"

(934字)

本文摘自沈之瑜:《甲骨文讲疏》,上海:上海书店出版社,2002年,第1—2页。

Task 1 Questions for Comprehension and Discussion

Directions: Please answer the following questions.

1. How was the ancient heritage of oracle bone script uncovered by accident?
2. What are the factors and elements that led to the discovery of the oracle bone script?
3. What significance does the discovery of the oracle bone script have?

Task 2 Summary

Directions: You are expected to tell your English-speaking friend the process and significance of the discovery of the oracle bone script. Write a summary of the above text in about 300 words in English for this purpose.

_____

_____

_____

_____

_____

Passage B

Formal and Substantive Universals of Languages[1]

(Excerpt)

Noam Chomsky[2]

A theory of linguistic structure that aims for explanatory adequacy incorporates an account of linguistic universals, and it attributes tacit knowledge of these universals to the child. It proposes, then, that the child approaches the data with the presumption that they are drawn from a language of a certain antecedently well-defined type, his problem being to determine which of the (humanly) possible languages is that of the community in which he is placed. Language learning would be impossible unless this were the case. The important question is: What are the initial assumptions concerning the nature of language that the child brings to language learning, and how detailed and specific is the innate schema (the general definition of "grammar") that gradually becomes more explicit and differentiated as the child learns the language? For the present we cannot come at all close to making a hypothesis about innate schemata that is rich, detailed, and specific enough to account for the fact of language acquisition. Consequently, the main task of linguistic theory must be to develop an account of linguistic universals that, on the one hand, will not be falsified by the actual diversity of languages and, on the other, will be sufficiently rich and explicit to account for the rapidity and uniformity of language learning, and the remarkable complexity and range of the generative grammars that are the product of language learning.

The study of linguistic universals is the study of properties of any generative grammar for a natural language. Particular assumptions about linguistic universals may pertain to either the syntactic, semantic, or phonological component, or to interrelations among the three components.

It is useful to classify linguistic universals as *formal* or *substantive*. A theory of substantive universals claims that items of a particular kind in any language must be drawn from a fixed class of items. For example, Jakobson's theory of distinctive features can be interpreted as making an assertion about substantive universals with respect to the phonological component of a generative grammar. It asserts that each output of this component consists of elements that are characterized in terms of some small number of fixed, universal, phonetic features (perhaps on the order of fifteen or twenty), each of which has a substantive acoustic-articulatory characterization independent of any particular language. Traditional universal grammar was also a theory of substantive universals, in this sense. It not only put forth interesting views as to the nature of universal phonetics, but also advanced the position that certain fixed syntactic categories (Noun, Verb, etc.) can be found in the syntactic representations of the sentences of any language, and that these provide the general underlying syntactic structure of each language. A theory of substantive semantic universals might hold for example, that certain designative functions must be carried out in a specified way in each language. Thus it might assert that each language will contain terms that designate persons or lexical items referring to certain specific kinds of objects, feelings, behavior, and so on.

It is also possible, however, to search for universal properties of a more abstract sort. Consider a claim that the grammar of every language meets certain specified formal conditions. The truth of this hypothesis would not in itself imply that any particular rule must appear in all or even in any two grammars. The property of having a grammar meeting a certain abstract condition might be called a *formal* linguistic universal, if shown to be a general property of natural languages. Recent attempts to specify the abstract conditions that a generative grammar must meet have produced a variety of proposals concerning formal universals, in this sense. For example, consider the proposal that the syntactic component of a grammar must contain transformational rules (these being operations of a highly special kind) mapping semantically interpreted deep structures into phonetically interpreted surface structure, or the proposal that the phonological component of a grammar consists of a sequence of rules, a subset of which may apply cyclically to successively more dominant constituents of the surface structure (a transformational cycle, in the sense of much recent work of phonology). Such proposals make claims of a quite different sort from the claim that certain substantive phonetic elements are available for phonetic representation in all languages, or that certain categories must be central to the syntax of all languages, or that certain semantic features or categories provide a universal framework for semantic description. Substantive universals such as these concern the vocabulary for the description of language; formal universals involve rather the character of the rules that appear in grammars and the ways in which they can be interconnected.

On the semantic level, too, it is possible to search for what might be called formal universals, in essentially the sense just described. Consider, for example, the assumption that proper names, in any language, must designate objects meeting a condition of spatiotemporal contiguity, and that the same is true of other terms designating objects; or the condition that the color words of any language must subdivide the color spectrum into continuous segments; or the condition that artifacts are defined in terms of certain human goals, needs, and functions instead of solely in terms of physical qualities. Formal constrains of this sort on a system of concepts may severely limit the choice (by the child, or the linguist) of a descriptive grammar, given primary linguistic data.

(892 words)

Notes

1. The text is excerpted from Noam Chomsky's *Aspects of the Theory of Syntax*. (The MIT Press, 1965, pp. 27-30).
2. Avram Noam Chomsky (born December 7, 1928) is an American linguist, philosopher, cognitive scientist, logician, political commentator, social justice activist, and anarcho-syndicalist advocate. Sometimes described as the "father of modern linguistics", Chomsky is also a major figure in analytic philosophy. He has spent most of his career at the Massachusetts Institute of Technology (MIT), where he is currently Professor Emeritus, and has authored over 100 books. He is a prominent cultural figure.

Task 1 Questions for Comprehension and Discussion

Directions: Please answer the following questions.

1. According to Chomsky, what are the formal and substantive universals of language?
2. Could you provide some examples to demonstrate your understanding of the concepts of formal and substantive universals of language?

Task 2 Summary

Directions: You know a friend is interested in Chomsky's theories on language and he or she has not yet read this particular piece on the formal and substantive universals of language. Write a summary of the main ideas of the above text in about 500 words in Chinese for the benefit of your friend.

_____

_____

_____

_____

_____

Unit 2

HISTORY AND CIVILIZATION

A talent for History may be said to be born with us, as our chief inheritance. In a certain sense all men are historians. Is not every memory written quite full with Annals, wherein joy and mourning, conquest and loss manifoldly alternate; and, with or without philosophy, the whole fortunes of one little inward Kingdom, and all its politics, foreign and domestic, stand ineffaceably recorded?

—*Thomas Carlyle*

Learning Objectives

Upon the completion of this unit, you should be able to:

Remembering & Understanding	★ master the spelling and usages of new words and phrases of text A and text B; ★ read text A and text B with full knowledge of their intended meaning;
Analyzing & Applying	★ make reference to the techniques and/or main ideas of text A and text B in your writing and discussion; ★ express complex ideas and emotions on the subject of history, civilization and culture in oral and written forms;
Evaluating & Creating	★ agree or disagree with others' opinions and ideas on the subject of history, civilization and culture; ★ reproduce texts in your own language to display the ability of cross-cultural communication; ★ give your view on the differences between Chinese and Western culture, for example, their views on wisdom, their communication styles.

Part One Lead-in

Section 1 Listening

Directions: Please fill in the blanks with words or sentences on the basis of what you have heard in the audio clip. Then discuss the following questions in pairs or groups.

Cultural Diversity and Assimilation in America: a Failure?

As the 1 _____ has come upon us that assimilation in this country was proceeding on lines very different from those we had marked out for it, we found ourselves 2 _____ those who were thwarting our prophecies. The truth became culpable. We blamed the war; we blamed the Germans. And then we discovered with a moral shock that these movements had been making great headway before the war even began. We found that the tendency, 3 _____ as it might be, has been for the national clusters of immigrants, as they became more and more firmly established and more and more prosperous, to cultivate more and more assiduously 4 _____ of their homelands. Assimilation, in other words, instead of washing out the memories of Europe, made them more and more 5 _____. Just as these clusters became more and more objectively American, so did they become more and more German or Scandinavian or Bohemian or Polish.

6. What are your impressions about America as a country of immigrants? Do you think it tolerates and enjoys cultural diversity and assimilation?
7. According to the recording, why does the American public consider the idea of "melting-pot" a failure?
8. What is the unpleasant truth about assimilation in America?
9. Are you generally convinced by what you have heard that cultural diversity and assimilation in America is a failure? Give your reasons.

Section 2 Watching

Directions: Please watch the video clip and discuss the following questions in pairs or groups.

Ancient Egypt

1. When and how was the tomb of Tutankhamen discovered?
2. What impact did the discovery of Tutankhamen's tomb make on the world?
3. Which part of the video, in terms of either its narrative or visual images, impresses you the most? Give your reasons.

Part Two Reading and Writing

Pre-Reading Questions

1. What do you know about Thomas Carlyle, his works and his ideas?

2. What do you think History is? Could you give a one-sentence definition?

Text A

On History[1]
(Excerpt)
Thomas Carlyle[2]

1   A talent for History may be said to be born with us, as our chief inheritance. In a certain sense all men are historians. Is not every memory written quite full with Annals, wherein joy and mourning, conquest and loss manifoldly alternate; and, with or without philosophy, the whole fortunes of one little inward Kingdom, and all its politics, foreign and domestic, stand *ineffaceably* recorded? Our very speech is curiously historical. Most men, you may observe, speak only to narrate; not in imparting what they have thought, which indeed were often a very small matter, but in exhibiting what they have undergone or seen, which is a quite unlimited one, do talkers *dilate*. *Cut* us *off* from Narrative, how would the stream of conversation, even among the wisest, *languish* into detached handfuls, and among the foolish utterly *evaporate*! Thus, as we do nothing but enact History, we say little but recite it: nay, rather, in that widest sense, our whole spiritual life is built thereon. For, strictly considered, what is all Knowledge too but recorded Experience, and a product of History; of which, therefore, Reasoning and Belief, no less than Action and Passion, are essential materials.

2   Under a limited, and the only practicable shape, History proper, that part of History which treats of remarkable action, has, in all modern as well as ancient times, ranked among the highest arts, and perhaps never stood higher than in these times of ours. For whereas, of old, the charm of History lay chiefly in gratifying our common appetite for the wonderful, for the unknown; and her office was but as that of a Minstrel and Story-teller, she has now further become a Schoolmistress, and professes to instruct in gratifying. Whether with the stateliness of that *venerable* character, she may not have taken up something of its *austerity* and *frigidity*; whether in the logical terseness of a Hume or Robertson, the graceful ease and gay pictorial heartiness of a Herodotus or Froissart may not be wanting, is not the question for us here. Enough that all learners, all inquiring minds of every order, are gathered round her footstool, and *reverently* pondering her lessons, as the true basis of Wisdom. Poetry, Divinity, Politics, Physics, have each their *adherents* and adversaries; each little guilt supporting a defensive and offensive war for its own special domain; while the domain of History is as a Free Emporium, where all these *belligerents* peaceably meet and furnish themselves; and Sentimentalist and Utilitarian, Sceptic and Theologian, with one voice advise us: Examine History, for it is "Philosophy teaching by Experience."

3 Far be it from us to *disparage* such teaching, the very attempt at which must be precious. Neither shall we too rigidly inquire: How much it has hitherto profited? Whether most of what little practical wisdom men have, has come from study of professed History, or from other less boasted sources, whereby, as matters now stand, a Marlborough may become great in the world's business with no History save what he derives from Shakespeare's Plays? Nay, whether in that same teaching by Experience, historical Philosophy has yet properly deciphered the first element of all science in this kind? What the aim and significance of that *wondrous* changeful Life it investigates and paints may be? Whence the course of man's destinies in this Earth originated, and whither they are tending? Or, indeed, if they have any course and tendency, are really guided forward by an unseen mysterious Wisdom, or only circle in blind mazes without recognizable guidance? Which questions, altogether fundamental, one might think, in any Philosophy of History, have, since the era when Monkish Annalists were *wont* to answer them by the long-ago extinguished light of their Missal and Breviary, been by most philosophical Historians only glanced at dubiously and from afar; by many, not so much as glanced at.

4 The truth is, two difficulties, never wholly surmountable, lie in the way. Before Philosophy can teach by Experience, the Philosophy has to be in readiness, the Experience must be gathered and intelligibly recorded. Now, overlooking the former consideration, and with regard only to the latter, let anyone who has examined the current of human affairs, and how intricate, perplexed, unfathomable, even when seen into with our own eyes, are their thousand-fold blending movements, say whether the true representing of it is easy or impossible. Social Life is the *aggregate* of all the individual men's Lives who constitute society; History is the essence of innumerable Biographies. But if one Biography, nay, our own Biography, study and recapitulate it as we may, remains in so many points unintelligible to us, how much more must these million, the very facts of which, to say nothing of the *purport* of them, we know not, and cannot know!

5 Neither will it adequately avail us to assert that the general inward condition of Life is the same in all ages; and that only the remarkable deviations from the common *endowment* and common lot, and the more important variations which the outward figure of Life has from time to time undergone, deserve memory and record. The inward condition of Life, it may rather be affirmed, the conscious or half-conscious aim of mankind, so far as men are not mere digesting-machines, is the same in no two ages; neither are the more important outward variations easy to fix on, or always well capable of representation. Which was the greater innovator, which was the more important personage in man's history—he who first led armies over the Alps, and gained the victories of Cannae and Thrasymene; or the nameless boor who first hammered out for himself an iron spade? When the oak-tree is felled, the whole forest echoes with it; but a hundred acorns are planted silently by some unnoticed breeze. Battles and war-*tumults*, which for the time din every ear, and with joy or terror

Unit 2

intoxicate every heart, pass away like tavern-brawls; and, except some few Marathons and Morgartens, are remembered by accident, not by desert.

Laws themselves, political Constitutions, are not our Life, but only the house wherein our Life is led: nay, they are but the bare walls of the house; all whose essential furniture, the inventions and traditions, the daily habits that regulate and support our existence, are the work not of Dracos and Hampdens, but of Phoenician mariners, of Italian masons and Saxon *metallurgists*, of philosophers, alchemists, prophets, and all the long-forgotten train of artists and artisans, who from the first have been jointly teaching us how to think and how to act, how to rule over spiritual and over physical Nature. Well may we say that of our History the more important part is lost without recovery; and—as thanksgivings were once wont to be offered "for unrecognized mercies"—look with reverence into the dark untenanted places of the Past, where, in formless oblivion, our chief benefactors, with all their *sedulous* endeavors, but not with the fruit of these, lie entombed.

So imperfect is that same Experience, by which Philosophy is to teach. Nay, even with regard to those occurrences which do stand recorded, which, at their origin have seemed worthy of record, and the summary of which constitutes what we now call History, is not our understanding of them altogether incomplete; is it even possible to represent them as they were? The old story of Sir Walter Raleigh's looking from his prison window on some street tumult, which afterwards three witnesses reported in three different ways, himself differing from them all, is still a true lesson to us.

(1257 words)

New Words

ineffaceably	[ˌɪnɪˈfeɪsəblɪ]	*adv.*	impossibly to be erased 不能消除地；不可抹去地，抹不掉地
dilate	[daɪˈleɪt]	*v.*	add details, as to an account or idea; clarify the meaning of and discourse in a learned way, usually in writing 扩大；膨胀；详述
languish	[ˈlæŋgwɪʃ]	*v.*	lose vigor, health, or flesh, as through grief; have a desire for something or someone who is not present 憔悴；凋萎；失去活力；苦思
evaporate	[ɪˈvæpəreɪt]	*v.*	lose or cause to lose liquid by vaporization leaving a more concentrated residue 蒸发，挥发；消失
venerable	[ˈven(ə)rəb(ə)l]	*adj.*	considered to deserve great respect or honour (used of someone or something old) 庄严的，值得尊敬的；珍贵的
austerity	[ɒˈsterɪtɪ]	*n.*	the trait of great self-denial (especially refraining from worldly pleasures) 朴素；苦行；严厉

frigidity	[frɪˈdʒɪdətɪ]	n.	a lack of affection or enthusiasm 冷淡；寒冷
reverently	[ˈrɛvərəntlɪ]	adv.	with reverence; in a reverent manner 虔诚地，恭敬地
adherent	[ədˈhɪər(ə)nt]	n.	someone who believes and helps to spread the doctrine of another 信徒；追随者
belligerent	[bəˈlɪdʒ(ə)r(ə)nt]	n.	someone who fights (or is fighting) 参加斗殴的人或集团
disparage	[dɪˈspærɪdʒ]	v.	express a negative opinion of 蔑视；毁谤
wondrous	[ˈwʌndrəs]	adj.	extraordinarily good; used especially as intensifiers 奇妙的；令人惊奇的；非常的
wont	[wəʊnt]	adj.	accustomed 习惯于
aggregate	[ˈæɡrɪɡət]	n.	a sum total of many heterogenous things taken together 合计；集合体；总计
purport	[pəˈpɔːt]	n.	the intended meaning of a communication 意义，主旨；意图
endowment	[ɪnˈdaʊm(ə)nt]	n.	If someone has an endowment of a particular quality or ability, they possess it as a natural quality or ability. 天赋；天生的气质（或才能）
tumult	[ˈtjuːmʌlt]	n.	a state of commotion and noise and confusion 骚动；骚乱；吵闹；激动
metallurgist	[məˈtælədʒɪst]	n.	an engineer trained in the extraction, refining, alloying and fabrication of metals 冶金学者；冶金家
sedulous	[ˈsedjʊləs]	adj.	marked by care and persistent effort 聚精会神的；勤勉的；勤苦工作的

New Expressions

cut off — to cut someone or something off means to separate them from things that they are normally connected with 隔离

Notes

1. The text is excerpted from Carlyle's *Historical Essays* published by University of California Press, pp.3-6.
2. Thomas Carlyle (4 December 1795—5 February 1881) was a Scottish philosopher, satirical writer, essayist, historian and teacher. Considered one of the most important social commentators of his time, he presented many lectures during his lifetime with certain acclaim in the Victorian era. One of those conferences resulted in his famous work *On Heroes, Hero-Worship, and the Heroic in History* where he explains that the key role in history lies in the actions of the "Great Man", claiming that "History is nothing but the biography of the Great Man".

Unit 2

Task 1 Generating the Outline

Directions: Please identify the thesis of the passage and the main point of each paragraph, and then find out how these points develop the thesis.

_____
_____
_____
_____
_____
_____
_____
_____
_____

Task 2 Understanding the Text

Directions: Please answer the following questions based on Text A.

1. How does the author manage to convince the reader of the relationship between History and Life?
2. What does Carlyle mean when he claims that "A talent for History may be said to be born with us"?
3. Compared with other domains such as Poetry and Politics, what is special about the domain of History?
4. What important points have Carlyle made on History? How far do you agree or disagree with them?
5. What are the two difficulties that lie in the way of learning History?
6. What true lesson does the anecdote of Sir Walter Raleigh tell us? Could you tell a similar story that you have experienced in life?

Task 3 Learning the Words

Directions: Please fill in the blanks in the sentences below with the words listed in the box. Change the forms if necessary.

| ineffaceable | dilate | disparage | evaporate | purport |

1. Conversely, we can also say that the development of society and culture has left _____ marks on the human body.
2. Some of the compounds in the oil _____, reducing their impact on the environment.
3. The drug is designed to help blood vessels _____, allowing more blood to flow to the heart.
4. And several studies _____ to show that playing violent video games raises aggression levels.
5. If you allow your partner to _____ you, expect to hear other damaging words. Whatever you are willing to accept is exactly what you're going to get.

Task 4 Translating the Sentences

Directions: Please translate the following sentences into Chinese.

1. Most men, you may observe, speak only to narrate; not in imparting what they have thought, which indeed were often a very small matter, but in exhibiting what they have undergone or seen, which is a quite unlimited one, do talkers dilate.

2. Whether with the stateliness of that venerable character, she may not have taken up something of its austerity and frigidity; whether in the logical terseness of a Hume or Robertson, the graceful ease and gay pictorial heartiness of a Herodotus or Froissart may not be wanting, is not the question for us here.

3. Poetry, Divinity, Politics, Physics, have each their adherents and adversaries; each little guilt supporting a defensive and offensive war for its own special domain; while the domain of History is as a Free Emporium, where all these belligerents peaceably meet and furnish themselves; and Sentimentalist and Utilitarian, Sceptic and Theologian, with one voice advise us: Examine History, for it is "Philosophy teaching by Experience."

4. When the oak-tree is felled, the whole forest echoes with it; but a hundred acorns are planted silently by some unnoticed breeze.

5. The old story of Sir Walter Raleigh's looking from his prison window on some street tumult, which afterwards three witnesses reported in three different ways, himself differing from them all, is still a true lesson to us.

Unit 2

Task 5 Writing Exercises

Directions: Please answer the following questions according to your understanding of the text.

What is the central idea of the essay? How does the author go about and argue for that idea? What examples does the author use to help illustrate his points?

_____
_____
_____

Directions: After reading Carlyle's essay, would you like to modify your own definition of history? Do you think history has different versions? What are the elements that make one version more popular than another? Put your ideas and opinions down in an essay of about 300 words.

_____
_____
_____

Part Three   Reading and Speaking

Pre-Reading Questions

1. What do you think are the essences of Chinese civilization?
2. In your mind, what are the factors that make a civilization superior?

Text B

Chinese and Western Civilization Contrasted
(*Excerpt*)
Bertrand Russell

There is at present in China a close contact between our civilization and that which is native to *the Celestial Empire*. It is still a doubtful question whether this contact will breed a new civilization better than either of its parents, or whether it will merely destroy the native culture and replace it by that of America. Contacts between different civilizations have often in the past proved to be landmarks in human progress. Greece learnt from Egypt, Rome from Greece, the Arabs from the Roman Empire, *mediaeval* Europe from the Arabs, and Renaissance Europe from the Byzantines. In many of these cases, the pupils proved better than their masters. In the case of China, if we regard the Chinese as the pupils, this may be the case again.

In fact, we have quite as much to learn from them as they from us, but there is far less chance of our learning it. If I treat the Chinese as our pupils, rather than vice versa, it is only because I fear we are unteachable.

2   Although there have been many wars in China, the natural outlook of the Chinese is very *pacifistic*. I do not know of any other country where a poet would have chosen, as Po-Chui did in one of the poems translated by Mr. Waley, called by him *The Old Man with the Broken Arm*, to make a hero of a recruit who *maimed* himself to escape military service. Their pacifism is rooted in their *contemplative* outlook, and in the fact that they do not desire to change whatever they see. They take a pleasure—as their pictures—in observing characteristic manifestations of different kinds of life, and they have no wish to reduce everything to a preconceived pattern. They have not the ideal of progress which dominates the Western nations, and affords a rationalization of our active impulses. Progress is, of course, a very modern ideal even with us; it is part of what we owe to science and industrialism. The cultivated conservative Chinese of the present day talk exactly as their earliest sages write. If one points out to them that this shows how little progress there has been, they will say: "Why seek progress when you already enjoy what is excellent?" At first, this point of view seems to a European unduly *indolent*; but gradually doubts *as to* one's own wisdom grow up, and one begins to think that much of what we call progress is only restless change, bringing us no nearer to any desirable goal.

3   It is interesting to contrast what the Chinese have sought in the West with what the West has sought in China. The Chinese in the West seek knowledge, in the hope—which I fear is usually vain—that knowledge may prove a gateway to wisdom. White men have gone to China with three motives: to fight, to make money, and to convert the Chinese to our religion. The last of these motives has the merit of being idealistic, and has inspired many heroic lives. But the soldier, the merchant, and the missionary are alike concerned to stamp our civilization upon the world; they are all three, in a certain sense, *pugnacious*. The Chinese have no wish to convert us to Confucianism; they say "religions are many, but reason is one," and with that they are content to let us go our way. They are good merchants, but their methods are quite different from those of European merchants in China, who are perpetually seeking concessions, *monopolies*, railways, and mines, and endeavouring to get their claims supported by gunboats. The Chinese are not, as a rule, good soldiers, because the causes for which they are asked to fight are not worth fighting for, and they know it. But that is only a proof of their reasonableness.

4   I think the tolerance of the Chinese is *in excess of* anything that Europeans can imagine from their experience at home. We imagine ourselves tolerant, because we are more so than our ancestors. But we still practice political and social *persecution*, and what is more, we are firmly persuaded that our civilization and our way of life are immeasurably better than any other, so that when we come across a nation like the Chinese, we are convinced that the kindest thing we can do to them is to make them

like ourselves. I believe this to be a profound mistake. It seemed to me that the average Chinaman, even if he is miserably poor, is happier than the average Englishman, and is happier because the nation is built upon a more humane and civilized outlook than our own. Restlessness and pugnacity not only cause obvious evils, but fill our lives with discontent, *incapacitate us for* the enjoyment of beauty, and make us almost incapable of the contemplative virtues. In this respect we have grown rapidly worse during the last hundred years. I do not deny that the Chinese go too far in the other direction; but for that very reason I think contact between East and West is likely to be fruitful to both parties. They may learn from us the indispensable minimum of practical efficiency, and we may learn from them something of that contemplative wisdom which has enabled them to persist while all the other nations of *antiquity* have perished.

5   When I went to China, I went to teach; but every day that I stayed I thought less of what I had to teach them and more of what I had to learn from them. Among Europeans who had lived a long time in China, I found this attitude not uncommon; but among those whose stay is short, or who go only to make money, it is sadly rare. It is rare because the Chinese do not *excel in* the things we really value—military *prowess* and industrial enterprise. But those who value wisdom or beauty, or even the simple enjoyment of life, will find more of these things in China than in the distracted and *turbulent* West, and will be happy to live where such things are valued. I wish I could hope that China, in return for our scientific knowledge, may give us something of her large tolerance and contemplative peace of mind.

(1061 words)

New Words

celestial	[sɪˈlestɪəl]	*adj.*	of or relating to the sky, of heaven or the spirit 天上的, 天空的
mediaeval	[ˌmedɪˈiːvl]	*adj.*	connected with the Middle Ages 中世纪
pacifistic	[pæsɪˈfɪstɪk]	*adj.*	opposed to war 和平主义的
maim	[meɪm]	*v.*	injure or wound seriously and leave permanent disfiguration or mutilation 使残废
contemplative	[kənˈtemplətɪv]	*adj.*	persistently or morbidly thoughtful 沉思的; 冥想的
indolent	[ˈɪnd(ə)l(ə)nt]	*adj.*	lazy 懒惰的
pugnacious	[pʌɡˈneɪʃəs]	*adj.*	ready and able to resort to force or violence 好斗的, 好战的
monopoly	[məˈnɒp(ə)li]	*n.*	exclusive control or possession of something 垄断; 垄断者; 专卖权

persecution	[pɜːsɪˈkjuːʃn]	*n.*	the act of persecuting (especially on the basis of race or religion)迫害；残害；虐待
incapacitated	[ˌɪnkəˈpæsɪˌteɪtɪd]	*adj.*	lacking in or deprived of strength or power 不能行动的
antiquity	[ænˈtɪkwɪtɪ]	*n.*	extreme oldness, an artifact surviving from the past 古物；古代的遗物
prowess	[ˈpraʊɪs]	*n.*	a superior skill that you can learn by study and practice and observation 英勇；超凡技术；卓越的技能
turbulent	[ˈtɜːbjʊl(ə)nt]	*adj.*	characterized by unrest or disorder or insubordination 骚乱的, 混乱的；狂暴的

the Celestial Empire	the Great Kingdom 天朝上国
as to	as for; concerning 说到，关于
in excess of	more than; beyond 超过；较……为多
incapacitate somebody for something	deprive somebody of the ability (to do something) 夺去某人做某事的能力
excel in	be excellent in 在某方面突出

Bertrand Russell, 3rd Earl Russell (18 May 1872—2 February 1970) was a British philosopher, logician, mathematician, historian, writer, social critic and political activist. At various points in his life he considered himself a liberal, a socialist, and a pacifist, but he also admitted that he had never been any of these in any profound sense. He was born in Monmouth shire, into one of the most prominent aristocratic families in Britain. He is considered one of the founders of analytic philosophy along with his predecessor Gottlob Frege, colleague G. E. Moore, and his protégé Ludwig Wittgenstein. He is widely held to be one of the 20th century's premier logicians. In 1950 Russell was awarded the Nobel Prize in Literature "in recognition of his varied and significant writings in which he champions humanitarian ideals and freedom of thought". The text is excerpted from his 1922 book *The Problem of China*.

Unit 2

Task 1   Questions for Comprehension

Directions: Please answer the following questions based on Text B.

1. Do you agree with Russell's observation about the close contact between different civilizations and his conclusion that pupils always exceed their teachers?
2. Is it true that the Chinese people have a contemplative outlook in which pacifism is rooted?
3. What do you think is the ideal of progress that dominates the Western nations? Do you think the Chinese nation has or had a different understanding about progress?
4. How far do you agree or disagree with Russell's claim that what the Chinese have sought in the West is contrasted with what the West has sought in China?
5. In what ways could the contact between East and West be fruitful to both parties?
6. According to Russell, what are the major differences between Chinese and Western civilization? What does Russell appreciate most about Chinese civilization?

Task 2   Questions for Discussion

Directions: Discuss the following questions in pairs or groups.

1. Where do you think East and West should meet? What can they learn from each other? Is the world today more integrated or divided?
2. Are the virtues Russell observed about the Chinese people still prevalent in Chinese society today?
3. What are the issues touched upon by the author? What are the main arguments? How far do you agree or disagree with the author?
4. Work out a list of possible arguments that are either for or against the following statement: Today scientific and industrial progress is the most important mission for the civilisation and development of a nation.
5. Exchange and discuss your opinions with others, and make a summary of the most important arguments made by the group.

Part Four   Cross Cultural Communication

Passage A

丝绸之路与文化交流

"丝绸之路"一词,是著名的德国地理学家李希霍芬提出的。19世纪70年代,李希霍芬在他的《中国》一书中,把"中国与河中地区以及中国与印度之间,以丝绸贸易为媒介的这条西域交通路线"叫作"丝绸之路"。之后,德国的东洋史学家阿尔巴特·赫尔曼在其名著《中国与叙利亚之间的古代丝绸之路》一文中主张,应该"把这一名称的涵义进而一直延到通向遥远西方叙利亚的道路上去"。赫尔曼的主张,得到西欧一些汉学家们的赞同。进入20世纪以后,随着中西关系史研究的深入,"丝绸之路"一词被中外学者广泛使用,并把古代丝绸贸易所达到的地区,都包括在丝绸之路的范围内。因而,"丝绸之路"就成为古代从长安(今陕西西安)出发,经中亚、西亚、南亚到欧洲、非洲等地的陆路通道的通称。丝绸之路不仅成为古代主要的陆上商贸通道,也是中西文化交流的"桥梁"。

文献记载和考古发掘都证明,中西经济文化交流早在张骞通西域之前就已存在,《逸周书·世俘解》记载"凡武王俘商归玉亿有百万",1976年,在商都安阳发掘的殷王武丁配偶"妇好"墓中有大批玉器,经鉴定大部分是新疆玉料。新疆是我国著名的产玉之区,其所产之玉为中原所用,可见新疆地区早就和内地发生了联系。

古代传说也向我们展示了古人对西方的了解和联系。成书于战国时期的《穆天子传》,叙述的就是周穆王西游的故事。周穆王名姬满,是西周的第五个君主,当他即位13年后,决定乘车西游。英俊潇洒的周穆王,乘坐八匹骏马拉着的马车,离开镐京(今西安),先东行到河南省,然后北上至今山西省滹沱河北岸,再折向西行,经内蒙溯黄河而上,过今宁夏、甘肃、青海后,进入今新疆地区,登昆仑山。又继续西行,到达今巴勒斯坦一带。相传穆王途经崦嵫山时,见到了他日夜思念的西王母,他赠给西王母许多丝织品和其他礼物,西王母也回赠了许多珍贵礼品。临别时,穆王在崦嵫山的瑶池举行盛大的答谢宴会,席间,西王母深情地对穆王说:"白云在天,山陵自出;道里悠远,山川间之。将子无死,尚能复来。"大意是说,蓝天上飘着白云,高高的山峰矗立于眼前。我们之间道路遥远,相隔千山万水,但愿你长生不老,有一天再来这里游玩。穆王十分感动,答应王母:"予归东土,和治诸夏,万民均平,吾顾见汝。比及三年,将复而野。"其意是说,我返回国土,首先治理好自己的国家,待到天下太平,万民安乐之时,我便再来与你相见。最多三年,我们还将在这里相逢。

(972字)

本文选自杨秀清编著:《华戎交会的都市——敦煌与丝绸之路》,兰州:甘肃人民出版社,2000年,第18—19页。

Task 1　Questions for Comprehension and Discussion

Directions: Please answer the following questions.

1. According to the text, what is the origin of the Silk Road?
2. What was the historical significance of the Silk Road?
3. Do you like the legendary story told here about Zhou Mu Wang and Queen Mother of the West (Xi Wangmu)? What purpose do legends and folklores serve?

Task 2　Summary

Directions: You are expected to tell your English-speaking friends what you have learned about the Silk Road. Write a summary of the main ideas of the above text in English in about 300 words for this purpose.

Passage B

The Process of Civilisation
William H. McNeill

Civilisations brought strangers together and separated classes of people living side by side into distinct semi-autonomous groupings. Priests and rulers, warriors and artisans, merchants and travellers, masters and servants lived very differently from one another, yet all depended on exchanges of goods and services, regulated by customary rules on the one hand and, on the other, by demographic and material limits on supply and demand.

As compared to primary communities, urban-based civilisations were (and still are) tumultuous and unstable social structures, but they were also more powerful, coordinating the actions of larger numbers of persons partly by obedience to deliberate commands, and partly by negotiated, more or less voluntary, exchanges of goods and services. Larger numbers working together, whether willingly or unwillingly, deliberately or inadvertently, had the same effect that cooperation within larger bands of more or less undifferentiated individuals had had at the beginning of human history. In other words, civilized forms of society exerted power over the natural environs and over much larger human numbers than more homogeneous societies were able to do. Ever since the first civilisations arose, civilized social complexity therefore tended to spread, until in our own time almost all humankind is caught up in a single global system, exchanging messages furiously fast and upsetting traditional ways of life almost everywhere.

An appropriately imaginative historian can hope to discern major landmarks in the civilizing process by focusing on breakthroughs in communication and transport that altered the range and flow of messages among human populations, and thereby accelerated the propagation of novelties far and wide that met human wishes or wants better than before.

When people first learned to use paddles and sails to propel rafts and boats, possibilities for long-range encounters opened up along the coasts of easily navigable seas. Almost certainly parts of Southeast Asia (and especially the offshore islands of Indonesia) were the principal sites of this breakthrough. A vague horizon for seafaring is established by the fact that people who reached Australia some 40,000 year ago (and perhaps even earlier than that) must have used some sort of floatation device to get there. But wooden rafts and ships seldom leave archaeological traces; and since melting glaciers subsequently raised sea levels substantially, early coastal settlements in Southeast Asia and everywhere else have been inundated.

Still, it seems clear that at an early time sailing vessels began to exploit the reversible monsoon winds to sail to and fro in Southeast Asia and along the shores of the Indian Ocean. Such seafaring was well developed by the time Sumerian records offer a glimpse of the sea network that connected the land of Sumer at the head of the Persian Gulf with Indus and Egyptian societies—and with a wider world of seagoing peoples beyond.

Sumerian cities, in fact, arose where this sea network connected up with a newer network of caravan portage. Donkeys, the first important caravan animal, were domesticated about seven thousand years ago; but since caravan management was almost as complicated as seafaring it presumably took a while for overland portage to become significant. But when local peoples learned that letting caravans pass for a negotiated protection fee assured a better supply of exotic and desirable items than plundering them did, overland portage across relatively long distances began to connect diverse populations more insistently than before. And it is surely not an accident that it was in Sumer, where an already ancient seagoing network intermeshed with a newly accessible hinterland, that the first cities arose between 4000 and 3000 BCE. Goods and ideas moved along these communications networks and, where they converged, the Sumerians were in an optimal position to pick and choose, elaborating and improving upon skills and knowledge coming from far and near.

Sumerian achievements, such as writing, metallurgy, wheeled vehicles, and an impressive religion, spread outward along the same networks. For example, on distant northern steppes Indo-European herdsmen accepted the Sumerian pantheon of seven high gods—sky, earth, thunderstorm, sun, moon, fresh water, and salt water. And, with subsequent adjustments, their Aryan, Greek, Latin, Celtic, German, and Slavic descendants carried this pagan pantheon with them into India and across Europe.

Similarly, wheeled vehicles, in the form of two-wheeled chariots, reached China by 1400 BCE and helped to consolidate the power of the Shang dynasty. But of all Sumerian innovations, their resort to writing was perhaps the most significant since it added a new dimension to information storage and retrieval. Being more capacious, enduring, and reliable than human memory, written records allowed priests and rulers to collect and disperse indefinitely large quantities of material goods according to deliberate rules. As a result, government became more powerful; commands became more enforcible, even at a distance; and coordinated effort among thousands and eventually millions of persons became routine.

(814 words)

The text is excerpted from "A Short History of Humanity" (2000) by William H. McNeill.

Task 1　Questions for Comprehension and Discussion

Directions: Please answer the following questions.

1. According to the text, how did civilisation bring strangers together?
2. Can you give some examples of breakthroughs in communication and transport that led to major landmarks in the civilizing process?

Task 2　Summary

Directions: A friend of yours is writing a paper on the process of civilisation but is unable to read English. Write a summary of the main ideas of the above text in about 500 words in Chinese to inform your friend of its content.

Unit 3

PHILOSOPHY AND LIFE

If all men were well off, if poverty and disease had been reduced to their lowest possible point, there would still remain much to be done to produce a valuable society; and even in the existing world the goods of the mind are at least as important as the goods of the body. It is exclusively among the goods of the mind that the value of philosophy is to be found; and only those who are not indifferent to these goods can be persuaded that the study of philosophy is not a waste of time.

—Bertrand Russell

Learning Objectives

Upon the completion of this unit, you should be able to:

Remembering & Understanding	★ master the new words in text A and text B; ★ grasp values of philosophy and meaning in life;
Analyzing & Applying	★ recognize and reconstruct arguments from the texts; ★ advance an argument of your own as required;
Evaluating & Creating	★ evaluate an argument for its rational strength; ★ write an argumentative essay relevant to the topic of this unit; ★ present the life and thoughts of a Chinese philosopher.

Part One Lead-in

Section 1 Listening

Directions: Please fill in the blanks with words or sentences on the basis of what you have heard in the audio clip. Then discuss the following questions in pairs or groups.

Problems of Philosophy

This view of philosophy appears to result, partly from a wrong conception of 1_____, partly from a wrong conception of 2_____ which philosophy strives to achieve. Physical science, through the medium of inventions, is useful to innumerable people who are wholly ignorant of it; thus the study of physical science is to be recommended, not only, or primarily, because of the effect on 3_____, but rather because of the effect on 4_____. Thus utility does not belong to philosophy. If the study of philosophy has any value at all for others than students of philosophy, it must be only 5_____, through its effects upon the lives of those who study it. It is in these effects, therefore, if anywhere, that the value of philosophy must be primarily sought.

6. What is the view of philosophy that Russell criticized?
7. Where did Russell think this view of philosophy derive from?
8. How does physical science differ from philosophy?
9. Where does the value of philosophy lie?

Section 2 Watching

Directions: Please watch the video clip and discuss the following questions in pairs or groups.

Zeno Paradox

1. What is the paradox Zeno came up with?
2. What implication does it have for mortgage payment?

Part Two Reading and Writing

Pre-Reading Questions

1. What is philosophy? This is a serious question in academic world as well as a common topic in ordinary life. Please give examples to show the ways in which the question can be answered variously.
2. What is philosophy for? Why do people study philosophy? Why do people read philosophy? Do you read philosophy? What do you expect to get from reading philosophy?
3. What do philosophers do? What do you think professors and students in philosophy are supposed to do in their capacity? How does their work differ from other academicians?

Unit 3

Text A

What Philosophy Is For
Bertrand Russell

1   Philosophy, like all other studies, aims primarily at knowledge. The knowledge it aims at is the kind of knowledge which gives unity and system to the body of the sciences, and the kind which *results from* a critical examination of the grounds of our *convictions*, prejudices, and beliefs. But it cannot be maintained that philosophy has had any very great measure of success in its attempts to provide definite answers to its questions. If you ask a mathematician, a mineralogist, a historian, or any other man of learning, what definite body of truths has been *ascertained* by his science, his answer will last *as long as* you are willing to listen. But if you put the same question to a philosopher, he will, if he is candid, have to confess that his study has not achieved positive results such as have been achieved by other sciences. It is true that this is partly *accounted for* by the fact that, as soon as definite knowledge concerning any subject becomes possible, this subject *ceases* to be called philosophy, and becomes a separate science. The whole study of the heavens, which now belongs to astronomy, was once included in philosophy; Newton's great work was called "the mathematical principles of natural philosophy". Similarly, the study of the human mind, which was a part of philosophy, has now been separated from philosophy and has become the science of psychology. Thus, to a great extent, the uncertainty of philosophy is more apparent than real: those questions which are already capable of definite answers are placed in the sciences, while those only to which, at present, no definite answer can be given, remain to form the residue which is called philosophy.

2   This is, however, only a part of the truth concerning the uncertainty of philosophy. There are many questions—and among them those that are of the profoundest interest to our spiritual life—which, so far as we can see, must remain *insoluble* to the human *intellect* unless its powers become of quite a different order from what they are now. Has the universe any unity of plan or purpose, or is it a *fortuitous* concourse of atoms? Is consciousness a permanent part of the universe, giving hope of indefinite growth in wisdom, or is it a transitory accident on a small planet on which life must ultimately become impossible? Are good and evil of importance to the universe or only to man? Such questions are asked by philosophy, and variously answered by various philosophers. But it would seem that, whether answers be otherwise discoverable or not, the answers suggested by philosophy are none of them *demonstrably* true. Yet, however slight may be the hope of discovering an answer, it is part of the business of philosophy to continue the consideration of such questions, to make us aware of their importance, to examine all the approaches to them, and to *keep alive* that speculative interest in the universe which *is apt to* be killed by confining

ourselves to definitely *ascertainable* knowledge.

3   Many philosophers, it is true, have held that philosophy could establish the truth of certain answers to such fundamental questions. They have supposed that what is of most importance in religious beliefs could be proved by strict demonstration to be true. In order to judge of such attempts, it is necessary to take a survey of human knowledge, and to form an opinion as to its methods and its limitations. On such a subject it would be unwise to pronounce dogmatically; but we shall be compelled to renounce the hope of finding philosophical proofs of religious beliefs. We cannot, therefore, include as part of the value of philosophy any definite set of answers to such questions. Hence, once more, the value of philosophy must not depend upon any supposed body of definitely ascertainable knowledge to be acquired by those who study it.

4   The value of philosophy is, in fact, to be sought largely in its very uncertainty. The man who has no *tincture* of philosophy goes through life imprisoned in the prejudices derived from common sense, from the habitual beliefs of his age or his nation, and from convictions which have grown up in his mind without the cooperation or *consent* of his deliberate reason. To such a man the world tends to become definite, finite, obvious; common objects *rouse* no questions, and unfamiliar possibilities are *contemptuously* rejected. As soon as we begin to philosophize, on the contrary, we find that even the most everyday things lead to problems to which only very incomplete answers can be given. Philosophy, though unable to tell us with certainty what is the true answer to the doubts which it raises, is able to suggest many possibilities which enlarge our thoughts and free them from the *tyranny* of custom. Thus, while diminishing our feeling of certainty as to what things are, it greatly increases our knowledge as to what they may be; it removes the somewhat *arrogant* dogmatism of those who have never traveled into the region of liberating doubt, and it keeps alive our sense of wonder by showing familiar things in an unfamiliar aspect.

5   *Apart from* its *utility* in showing unsuspected possibilities, philosophy has a value—perhaps its chief value—through the greatness of the objects which it contemplates, and the freedom from narrow and personal aims resulting from this *contemplation*. The life of the instinctive man is shut up within the circle of his private interests: family and friends may be included, but the outer world is not regarded except as it may help or hinder what comes within the circle of instinctive wishes. In such a life there is something feverish and confined, *in comparison with* which the philosophic life is calm and free. The private world of instinctive interests is a small one, set in the midst of a great and powerful world which must, sooner or later, lay our private world in ruins. Unless we can so enlarge our interests as to include the whole outer world, we remain like a *garrison* in a *beleaguered* fortress, knowing that the enemy prevents escape and that ultimate surrender is inevitable. In such a life there is no peace, but a constant *strife* between the insistence of desire and the powerlessness of will. In one way or another, if our life is to be great and free, we must escape this prison and this strife.

Unit 3

Thus, to sum up our discussion of the value of philosophy; Philosophy is to be studied, not *for the sake of* any definite answers to its questions since no definite answers can, as a rule, be known to be true, but rather for the sake of the questions themselves; because these questions enlarge our conception of what is possible, enrich our intellectual imagination and diminish the dogmatic assurance which closes the mind against *speculation*; but *above all* because, through the greatness of the universe which philosophy contemplates, the mind also is *rendered* great, and becomes capable of that union with the universe which constitutes its highest good.

(1182 words)

New Words

conviction	[kən'vɪkʃən]	*n.*	an unshakable belief in something without need for proof or evidence 确信, 确定的信仰
ascertain	[ˌæsə'teɪn]	*v.*	establish after a calculation, investigation, experiment, survey, or study 确定, 查明
cease	[si:s]	*v.*	put an end to a state or an activity 停止, 结束
insoluble	[ɪn'sɔljubl]	*adj.*	without hope of solution 不能解决的
intellect	['ɪntəlekt]	*n.*	knowledge and intellectual ability 智力, 理解力
fortuitous	[fɔ:'tjuːɪtəs]	*adj.*	occurring by happy chance 偶然的, 意外的
demonstrably	['demənstrəblɪ]	*adv.*	in an obvious and provable manner 可论证地, 明确地
ascertainable	[ˌæsə'teɪnəbl]	*adj.*	capable of being ascertained or found out 可查明的, 可确定的
tincture	['tɪŋktʃə]	*n.*	an indication that something has been present 迹象
consent	[kən'sent]	*n.*	permission to do something 同意
rouse	[rauz]	*v.*	cause to become awake or conscious 唤醒, 激起
contemptuously	[kən'temptjuəslɪ]	*adv.*	without respect; in a disdainful manner 轻蔑地
tyranny	['tɪrənɪ]	*n.*	a form of government in which the ruler is an absolute dictator (not restricted by a constitution or laws or opposition, etc.) 暴政, 专横
arrogant	['ærəgənt]	*adj.*	having or showing feelings of unwarranted importance out of overbearing pride 自大的, 傲慢的
utility	[ju:'tɪlətɪ]	*n.*	the quality of being of practical use 效用, 功用
contemplation	[ˌkɔntem'pleɪʃən]	*n.*	a calm lengthy intent consideration 沉思
garrison	['gærɪsən]	*n.*	a fortified military post where troops are stationed 要塞
beleaguer	[bɪ'li:gə]	*v.*	surround so as to force to give up 围攻
strife	[straɪf]	*n.*	bitter conflict; heated often violent dissension 冲突
speculation	[ˌspekju'leɪʃən]	*n.*	a hypothesis that has been formed by speculating or conjecturing (usually with little hard evidence) 推测

| render | [ˈrendə] | v. | cause to become 致使 |

New Expressions

result from	arise from, root in 起因于
as long as	on condition 只要
account for	give reasons for 对……做出解释
keep alive	maintain the vigor and vitality 保持生机
be apt to	tend to be 倾向于
apart from	to refer to something, often something small or unimportant, which is an exception to the general situation or state of affairs 除……之外,且不说
in comparison with	in contrast with 相比之下
for the sake of	in the cause of 为了
above all	above and beyond all other consideration 尤其是

The text is excerpted from Chapter XV of *The Problems of Philosophy*.

Task 1   Generating the Outline

Directions: Please identify the thesis of the passage and the main point of each paragraph, and then find out how these points develop the thesis.

_____
_____
_____
_____
_____
_____
_____
_____

Unit 3

Task 2 Understanding the Text

Directions: Please answer the following questions based on Text A.

1. According to the author, what is the similarity between philosophy and science?
2. How does philosophy contribute to science in terms of knowledge?
3. Where does philosophical knowledge come from?
4. What fact can be adduced to account for why philosophy has not had any very great measure of success in its attempts to provide definite answers to its questions?
5. What examples have been adduced to show that, whenever definite answers can be given to certain questions in a subject, that subject would not be called philosophy but become a separate science?
6. Why does the author say "the uncertainty of philosophy is more apparent than real"?
7. What questions are insoluble to the human intellect according to the author?
8. What is philosophy supposed to do in dealing with the insoluble questions facing human beings?
9. What attitudes do we need to take towards the insoluble questions like religious beliefs?
10. Where does the author think the prejudice of a man with no tincture of philosophy come from?
11. What are the differences between a person who philosophizes and the one who does not philosophize?
12. What does philosophy enable us to do if it is unable to provide definite answers to the questions it raises?
13. What is the life of the instinctive man like, as compared with the philosophic life?
14. What can we learn from the author about the value of philosophy?

Task 3 Learning the Phrases

Directions: Please fill in the blanks in the sentences below with the phrases listed in the box. Change the forms if necessary.

| aim at | as long as | account for | aware of | for the sake of |

1. It is the business of the scientist to accumulate knowledge about the universe and all that is in it, and to find, if he is able, common factors which underlie and _____ the facts that he knows.
2. Why, in its presence, should I deny the joy of living, _____ I know everything is not included in this joy?
3. Most of our educational traditions _____ wisdom.
4. I need not press the urgency of the matter on you, as I know you are fully _____ it yourselves.
5. _____ keeping things simple, we'll stick to the models that seem truly promising.

Task 4 Translating the Sentences

Directions: Please translate the following sentences into Chinese.

1. Thus, to a great extent, the uncertainty of philosophy is more apparent than real: those questions which are already capable of definite answers are placed in the sciences, while those only to which, at present, no definite answer can be given, remain to form the residue which is called philosophy.

2. There are many questions—and among them those that are of the profoundest interest to our spiritual life—which, so far as we can see, must remain insoluble to the human intellect unless its powers become of quite a different order from what they are now.

3. Yet, however slight may be the hope of discovering an answer, it is part of the business of philosophy to continue the consideration of such questions, to make us aware of their importance, to examine all the approaches to them, and to keep alive that speculative interest in the universe which is apt to be killed by confining ourselves to definitely ascertainable knowledge.

4. The man who has no tincture of philosophy goes through life imprisoned in the prejudices derived from common sense, from the habitual beliefs of his age or his nation, and from convictions which have grown-up in his mind without the cooperation or consent of his deliberate reason.

5. Philosophy is to be studied, not for the sake of any definite answers to its questions since no definite answers can, as a rule, be known to be true, but rather for the sake of the questions themselves.

Task 5 Writing Exercises

Directions: Please find a philosopher (a teacher or a student who is doing philosophy) for an interview on what philosophy is about.

Unit 3

Directions: What do you think of the relation between philosophy and science? Write an essay discussing how philosophy relates to science.

_____

_____

_____

Part Three   Reading and Speaking

Pre-Reading Questions

1. Could you give examples to show what a meaningful life is like?
2. How could a person's life be meaningful?

Text B

Meaning in Life[1]
Susan Wolf[2]

A meaningful life is, *first of all*, one that has within it the basis for an *affirmative* answer to the needs or longings that are *characteristically* described as needs for meaning. I have in mind, for example, the sort of questions people ask on their deathbeds, or simply in contemplation of their eventual deaths, about whether their lives have been (or are) worth living, whether they have had any point, and the sort of questions one asks when considering suicide and wondering whether one has any reason to go on.

To what general characteristics of meaningfulness do these images lead us and how do they provide an answer to the longings mentioned above? Roughly, I would say that meaningful lives are lives of active *engagement* in projects of worth. Of course, a good deal needs to be said in elaboration of this statement. Let me begin by discussing the two key phrases, "active engagement" and "projects of worth."

A person is actively engaged by something if she is gripped, excited, involved by it. Most obviously, we are actively engaged by the things and people about which and whom we are passionate. Opposites of active engagement are boredom and *alienation*. To be actively engaged in something is not always pleasant in the ordinary sense of the word. Activities in which people are actively engaged frequently involve stress, danger, *exertion*, or sorrow (consider, for example: writing a book, climbing a mountain, training for a marathon, caring for an ailing friend). However, there is something good about the feeling of engagement: one feels (typically without thinking about it) especially alive.

4 That a meaningful life must involve "projects of worth" will, I expect, be more *controversial*, for the phrase hints of a *commitment* to some sort of objective value. This is not accidental, for I believe that the idea of meaningfulness, and the concern that our lives possess it, are conceptually linked to such a commitment. Indeed, it is this linkage that I want to defend, for I have neither a philosophical theory of what objective value is nor a substantive theory about what has this sort of value. What is clear to me is that there can be no sense to the idea of meaningfulness without a distinction between more and less worthwhile ways to spend one's time, where the test of worth is at least partly independent of a subject's ungrounded preferences or enjoyment.

5 Consider first the longings or concerns about meaning that people have, their wondering whether their lives are meaningful, their vows to add more meaning to their lives. The sense of these concerns and *resolves* cannot fully be captured by an account in which what one does with one's life doesn't matter, as long as one enjoys or prefers it. Sometimes people have concerns about meaning despite their knowledge that their lives *to date* have been satisfying. Indeed, their enjoyment and "active engagement" with activities and values they now see as shallow seems only to heighten the sense of meaninglessness that comes to *afflict* them. Their sense that their lives so far have been meaningless cannot be a sense that their activities have not been chosen or fun. When they look for sources of meaning or ways to add meaning to their lives, they are searching for projects whose *justifications* lie elsewhere.

6 Second, we need an explanation for why certain sorts of activities and involvements come to mind as contributors to meaningfulness while others seem intuitively inappropriate. Think about what gives meaning to your own life and the lives of your friends and acquaintances. Among the things that tend to come up on such lists, I have already mentioned moral and intellectual accomplishments and the ongoing activities that lead to them. Relationships with friends and relatives are perhaps even more important for most of us. *Aesthetic* enterprises (both creative and appreciative), the cultivation of personal virtues, and religious practices frequently loom large. *By contrast*, it would be odd, if not bizarre, to think of crossword puzzles, sitcoms, or the kind of computer games to which I am fighting off addiction as providing meaning in our lives, though there is no question that they afford a sort of satisfaction and that they are the objects of choice. Some things, such as chocolate and aerobics class, I choose even at considerable cost to myself (it is irrelevant that these particular choices may be related), so I must find them worthwhile in a sense. But they are not the sorts of things that make life worth living.

7 "Active engagement in projects of worth," I suggest, answers to the needs an account of meaningfulness in life must meet. If a person is or has been thus actively engaged, then she does have an answer to the question of whether her life is or has been worthwhile, whether it has or has had a point. When someone looks for ways to

add meaning to her life, she is looking (though perhaps not under this description) for worthwhile projects about which she can get *enthused*. The account also explains why some activities and projects but not others come to mind as contributors to meaning in life. Some projects, or *at any rate*, particular acts, are worthwhile but too boring or mechanical to be sources of meaning. Other acts and activities, though highly pleasurable and deeply involving, do not seem to have the right kind of value to contribute to meaning.

8   Roughly, then, according to my proposal, a meaningful life must satisfy two criteria, suitably linked. First, there must be active engagement, and second, it must be engagement in (or with) projects of worth. A life is meaningless if it lacks active engagement with anything. A person who is bored or alienated from most of what she spends her life doing is one whose life can be said to lack meaning. Note that she may in fact be performing functions of worth. At the same time, someone who is actively engaged may also live a meaningless life, if the objects of her involvement are utterly worthless.

9   We may summarize my proposal in terms of a slogan: "Meaning arises when subjective attraction meets objective attractiveness." The idea is that in a world in which some things are more worthwhile than others, meaning arises when a subject discovers or develops an *affinity* for one or typically several of the more worthwhile things and has and makes use of the opportunity to engage with it or them in a positive way.

(1087 words)

New Words

affirmative	[əˈfɜːmətɪv]	*adj.*	affirming or giving assent 肯定的，积极的
characteristically	[ˌkærɪktəˈrɪstɪklɪ]	*adv.*	in characteristic manner 典型地，表示特性地
engagement	[ɪnˈɡeɪdʒmənt]	*n.*	the act of sharing in the activities of a group 交融
alienation	[ˌeɪljəˈneɪʃən]	*n.*	the feeling of being alienated from other people 异化，疏远
exertion	[ɪɡˈzɜːʃən]	*n.*	use of physical or mental energy; hard work 发挥，运用，努力
controversial	[ˌkɒntrəˈvɜːʃəl]	*adj.*	marked by or capable of arousing controversy 有争议的
commitment	[kəˈmɪtmənt]	*n.*	the act of binding yourself (intellectually or emotionally) to a course of action 承担义务
resolve	[rɪˈzɒlv]	*n.*	the trait of being resolute 决定要做的事
afflict	[əˈflɪkt]	*v.*	cause great unhappiness for; distress 折磨

justification	[ˌdʒʌstɪfɪˈkeɪʃən]	n.	a statement in explanation of some action or belief 理由,辩护
aesthetic	[iːsˈθetɪk]	adj.	concerning or characterized by an appreciation of beauty or good taste 美的,审美的
enthuse	[ɪnˈθjuːz]	v.	cause to feel enthusiasm 使热心
affinity	[əˈfɪnətɪ]	n.	a natural attraction or feeling of kinship 密切关系

New Expressions

first of all	before anything else 首先
engage in	employ oneself in 从事(于)
to date	prior to the present time 迄今为止
by contrast	by comparison 相比之下
at any rate	in any case 无论如何,至少

Notes

1. The text is excerpted from "Happiness and Meaning: Two Aspects of the Good Life" in *Social Philosophy and Policy* 14(01): 207, 1997.

2. Susan Wolf (born 1952) is a moral philosopher and philosopher of action who is currently the Edna J. Koury Professor of Philosophy at the University of North Carolina at Chapel Hill. She is a Fellow of the American Academy of Arts and Sciences and the American Philosophical Society, and received a Mellon Distinguished Achievement Award in the Humanities in 2002.

Task 1 Questions of Comprehension

Directions: Please answer the following questions based on Text B.

1. How does the author characterize a meaningful life?
2. How does the author account for active engagement?
3. How does the author understand projects of worth?
4. Active engagement in projects of worth, as an account, contributes to our understanding of meaningfulness in life. How does the author explicate this point?
5. How does the author summarize his position?

Task 2 Questions for Discussion

Directions: Discuss the following questions in pairs or groups.

1. Do you think your life is meaningful? How do you account for meaningfulness of your life?
2. Discuss the meaning in life with your partner(s).

Unit 3

Part Four Cross Cultural Communication

Passage A

中国哲学的线索

胡适

中国哲学到了老子和孔子的时候,才可当得"哲学"两个字。老子以前,不是没有思想,没有系统的思想;大概多是对于社会上不安宁的情形,发些牢骚语罢了。如《诗经》上说:"苕之华,其叶青青。知我如此,不如无生。"这种语是表示对于时势不满意的意思。到了西历前第六世纪时,思想家才对于社会上和政治上,求根本弊端所在。而他们的学说议论终是带有破坏的、批评的、革命的性质。老子根本上不满意当时的社会、政治、伦理、道德。原来人人多信"天"是仁的,而他偏说:"天地不仁,以万物为刍狗。"天是没有意思的,不为人类做好事的。他又主张废弃仁义,人于"无为而无不为"的境界。这种极破坏的思想,自然要引起许多反抗。孔子是老子的门徒或是朋友。他虽不满意于当时风俗制度以及事事物物,可是不取破坏的手段,不主张革命。他对于第一派是调和的、修正的、保守的。老子一派对于社会上无论什么政治、法律、宗教、道德,都不要了,都要推翻它,取消它。孔子一派平和一点,只求修正当时的制度。中国哲学的起点,有了这两个系统出来之后,内的线索——就是方法——继续变迁,却逃不出这两种。

老子的方法是无名的方法。《老子》第一句话就说:"名可名,非常名;道可道,非常道。"他知道"名"的重要,亦知道"名"的坏处,所以主张"无名"。名实二字在东西各国哲学史上都很重要。"名"是共相(universal),亦就是普通性。"实"是"自相",亦就是个性。名实两观念代表两大问题。从思想上研究社会的人,一定研究先从社会下手呢,还是从个人下手?换句话讲,是先决个性,还是先决普通之问题?"名"的重要可以举例明之。譬如诸君现在听讲,忽然门房跑来说——张先生,你的哥哥来了。这些代表思想的语言文字就是"名"。——倘若没有这些"名",他不能传达他的意思,诸君也无从领会他的意思,彼此就很觉困难了。简单的知识,非"名"无从表它,复杂的格外要藉"名"来表示它。"名"是知识上的问题,没有"名"便没有"共相"。而老子反对知识,便反对"名",反对言语文字,都要一个个地毁灭它。毁灭之后,一切人都无知无识,没有思想。没有思想,则没有欲望。没欲望,则不"为非作恶",返于太古时代浑朴状态了。这第一派的思想,注重个性而毁弃普遍。所以他说:"天下皆知美之为美,斯恶已;皆知善之为善,斯不善矣。"美和不美都是相对的,有了这个,便有那个。这个那个都不要,都取消,便是最好。这叫做"无名"的方法。

孔子处世之后,亦看得"名"很重要。不过他以为与其"无名",不如"正名"。

《论语·子路篇》说:

> 子路曰:卫君待子而为政,子将奚先?子曰:必也正名乎。子路曰:有是哉!子之迂也!奚其正!子曰:野哉由也!君子于其所不知,盖阙如也。名不正,则言不顺。言不顺,则事不成。事不成,则礼乐不兴。礼乐不兴,则刑罚不中。刑罚不中,则民无所措手足。

孔子以为"名"——语言文字——是不可少的,只要把一切文字、制度,都回复到他本来的理想标准,例如:"政者,正也。""仁者,人也。"他的理想的社会,便是"君君、臣臣、父父、子子"。做父亲的要做到父亲的理想标准,做儿子的亦要做到儿子的理想标准。社会上事事物物,都要做到这一步境地。

倘使君不君、臣不臣、父不父、子不子,则君、臣、父、子都失掉本来的意义了。怎样说"名不正,则言不顺"呢?"言"是"名"组成的,名字的意义,没有正当的标准,便连话都说不通了。孔子说:"觚不觚,觚哉觚哉!"觚是有角的形,故有角的酒器,叫做"觚"。后来把觚字用泛了,没有角的酒器亦叫做"觚"。所以孔子说:"现在觚没有角了,这还是觚吗?这还是觚吗?"不是觚的都叫做觚,这就是"言不顺"。现在通用的小洋角子,明明是圆的,偏叫它"角",也是同样的道理。语言文字(名)是代表思想的符号。语言文字没有正确的意义,便没有公认的是非真假的标准。要建设一种公认的是非真假的标准,所以他主张"正名"。老子主"无名",孔子主"正名"。此后思想,凡属老子一派的,便要推翻一切制度,便要讲究制度文物,压抑个人。

(1612字)

本文选自《教育杂志》第十三卷第十一号(1921年11月20日)。这是胡适1921年7月23日在商务印书馆开办的国语讲习所的讲演,大旨是说哲学的内部线索就是哲学方法的变迁。找出方法的变迁,则可得古今思想沿革的线索,这是研究中国哲学的目的之一。

Task 1 Questions for Comprehension and Discussion

Directions: Please answer the following questions.

1. How did Hu Shish compare Confucius with Laozi?
2. Interpret "无名" and "正名".

Task 2 Summary

Directions: Suppose you have been back from Hu Shish's lecture. Please write a summary in 300 words in English detailing Hu Shish's account of the development of Chinese philosophy? How do you compare Confucius with Laozi regarding their positions in Chinese philosophy?

Passage B

What Is Enlightenment?

Immanuel Kant

Enlightenment is man's emergence from his self-imposed nonage. Nonage is the inability to use one's own understanding without another's guidance. This nonage is self-imposed if its cause lies not in lack of understanding but in indecision and lack of courage to use one's own mind without another's guidance. *Dare to know!* (*Sapere aude.*) "Have the courage to use your own understanding," is therefore the motto of the enlightenment.

Laziness and cowardice are the reasons why such a large part of mankind gladly remain minors all their lives, long after nature has freed them from external guidance. They are the reasons why it is so easy for others to set themselves up as guardians. It is so comfortable to be a minor. If I have a book that thinks for me, a pastor who acts as my conscience, a physician who prescribes my diet, and so on—then I have no need to exert myself. I have no need to think, if only I can pay; others will take care of that disagreeable business for me. Those guardians who have kindly taken supervision upon themselves see to it that the overwhelming majority of mankind—among them the entire fair sex—should consider the step to maturity, not only as hard, but as extremely dangerous. First, these guardians make their domestic cattle stupid and carefully prevent the docile creatures from taking a single step without the leading-strings to which they have fastened them. Then they show them the danger that would threaten them if they should try to walk by themselves. Now this danger is really not very great; after stumbling a few times they would, at last, learn to walk. However, examples of such failures intimidate and generally discourage all further attempts.

Thus it is very difficult for the individual to work himself out of the nonage which has become almost second nature to him. He has even grown to like it, and is at first really incapable of using his own understanding because he has never been permitted to try it. Dogmas and formulas, these mechanical tools designed for reasonable use—or rather abuse—of his natural gifts, are the fetters of an everlasting nonage. The man who casts them off would make an uncertain leap over the narrowest ditch, because he is not used to such free movement. That is why there are only a few men who walk firmly, and who have emerged from nonage by cultivating their own minds.

It is more nearly possible, however, for the public to enlighten itself; indeed, if it is only given freedom, enlightenment is almost inevitable. There will always be a few independent thinkers, even among the self-appointed guardians of the multitude. Once such men have thrown off the yoke of nonage, they will spread about them the spirit of a reasonable appreciation of man's value and of his duty to think for himself. It is especially to be noted that the public which was earlier brought under the yoke by these men afterwards forces these very guardians to remain in submission, if it is so incited by some of its guardians who are themselves incapable of any enlightenment. That shows how pernicious it is to implant prejudices: they will eventually revenge themselves upon their authors or their authors' descendants. Therefore, a public can achieve enlightenment only slowly. A revolution may bring about the end of a personal despotism or of avaricious tyrannical oppression, but never a true reform of modes of thought. New prejudices will serve, in place of the old, as guide lines for the unthinking multitude.

This enlightenment requires nothing but *freedom*—and the most innocent of all that may be called "freedom": freedom to make public use of one's reason in all matters. Now I hear the cry from all sides: "Do not argue!" The officer says: "Do not argue—drill!" The tax collector: "Do not argue—pay!" The pastor: "Do not argue—believe!" Only one ruler in the world says: "Argue as much as you please, but obey!" We find restrictions on freedom everywhere. But which restriction is harmful to enlightenment? Which restriction is innocent, and which advances enlightenment? I reply: the public use of one's reason must be free at all times, and this alone can bring enlightenment to mankind.

On the other hand, the private use of reason may frequently be narrowly restricted without especially hindering the progress of enlightenment. By "public use of one's reason" I mean that use which a man, as *scholar*, makes of it before the reading public. I call "private use" that use which a man makes of his reason in a civic post that has been entrusted to him. In some affairs affecting the interest of the community a certain [governmental] mechanism is necessary in which some members of the community remain passive. This creates an artificial unanimity which will serve the fulfillment of public objectives, or at least keep these objectives from being destroyed. Here arguing is not permitted: one must obey. Insofar as a part of this machine considers himself at the same time a member of a universal community—a world society of citizens—(let us say that he thinks of himself as a scholar rationally addressing his public through his writings) he may indeed argue, and the affairs with which he is associated in part as a passive member will not suffer. Thus it would be very unfortunate if an officer on duty and under orders from his superiors should want to criticize the appropriateness or utility of his orders. He must obey. But as a scholar he could not rightfully be prevented from taking notice of the mistakes in the military service and from submitting his views to his public for its judgment. The citizen cannot refuse to pay the taxes levied upon him; indeed, impertinent censure of such taxes could be punished as a scandal that might cause general disobedience. Nevertheless, this man does not violate the duties of a citizen if, as a scholar, he publicly expresses his objections to the impropriety or possible injustice of such levies. A pastor, too, is bound to preach to his congregation in accord with the doctrines of the church which he serves, for he was ordained on that condition. But as a scholar he has full freedom, indeed the obligation, to communicate to his public all his carefully examined and constructive thoughts concerning errors in that doctrine and his proposals concerning improvement of religious dogma and church institutions. This is nothing that could burden his conscience. For what he teaches in pursuance of his office as representative of the church, he represents as something which he is not free to teach as he sees it. He speaks as one who is employed to speak in the name and under the orders of another. He will say: "Our church teaches this or that; these are the proofs which it employs." Thus he will benefit his congregation as much as possible by presenting doctrines to which he may not subscribe with full conviction. He can commit himself to teach them because it is not completely impossible that they may contain hidden truth. In any event, he has found nothing in the doctrines that contradicts the heart of religion. For if he believed that such contradictions existed he would not be able to administer his office with a clear conscience. He would have to resign it. Therefore the use which a scholar makes of his reason before the congregation that employs him is only a private use, for no matter how sizable, this is only a domestic audience. In view of this he, as preacher, is not free and ought not to be free, since he is carrying out the orders of others. On the other hand, as the scholar who speaks to his own public (the world) through his writings, the minister in the public use of his reason enjoys unlimited freedom to use his own reason and to speak for himself. That the spiritual guardians of the people should themselves be treated as minors is an absurdity which would result in perpetuating absurdities.

(1358 words)

Unit 3

 **Notes**

This is a 1784 essay by the philosopher Immanuel Kant. In the December 1784 publication of the *Berlinische Monatsschrift* (*Berlin Monthly*), edited by Friedrich Gedike and Johann Erich Biester, Kant replied to the question posed a year earlier by the Reverend Johann Friedrich Zöllner, who was also an official in the Prussian government. Zöllner's question was addressed to a broad intellectual public, in reply to Biester's essay entitled: "Proposal, not to engage the clergy any longer when marriages are conducted" (April 1783) and a number of leading intellectuals replied with essays, of which Kant's is the most famous and has had the most impact. Kant's opening paragraph of the essay is a much-cited definition of a lack of Enlightenment as people's inability to think for themselves due not to their lack of intellect, but lack of courage.

Kant's essay also addressed the causes of a lack of enlightenment and the preconditions necessary to make it possible for people to enlighten themselves. He held it necessary that all church and state paternalism be abolished and people be given the freedom to use their own intellect. Kant praised Frederick II of Prussia for creating these preconditions. Kant focused on religious issues, saying that "our rulers" had less interest in telling citizens what to think in regard to artistic and scientific issues.

Task 1   Questions for Comprehension and Discussion

Directions: Please answer the following questions.

1. What is Kant's definition of enlightenment?
2. What is public use of reason? What is private use of reason?

Task 2   Summary

Directions: Suppose your philosophy professor assigns a task of writing a review based on this essay. Please summarize the main idea of this essay in Chinese.

MUSIC AND THE SOCIAL WORLD

Composers—even great composers writing great works—create for people. Aware of a given society's values and behaviors, they calculate the place of their new composition in its world.

—*Thomas Forrest Kelly*

Learning Objectives

Upon the completion of this unit, you should be able to:

Remembering & Understanding	★ get to know better how works of art have stood the test time and become essential and formative parts of the web of human achievement; ★ be aware of the close connection between music and the social world;
Analyzing & Applying	★ identify unique perspectives and develop in-depth thinking; ★ write with better coherence and unity; ★ make an effective refutation;
Evaluating & Creating	★ get to know how traditional Chinese culture has a profound impact on the products of human creativity; ★ make a comparison between the roots of Western and Chinese music.

Unit 4

Part One Lead-in

Section 1 Listening

Directions: Please fill in the blanks with words or sentences on the basis of what you have heard in the audio clip. Then discuss the following questions in pairs or groups.

Preference for Familiar or Unfamiliar Sounds?

Saying that endless variety exists in music might seem unnecessary, yet many of us listen only to the sounds that have been made popular in our 1 _____: sounds on the majority of television and radio stations, on movie tracks, at pop concerts. Exploring unfamiliar sounds, finding perhaps the one radio station (among fifty others) dedicated to music that is new to us, refusing to have our tastes 2 _____: these actions we are free to perform yet too often we do not.

Popular music, that which we find 3 _____, is listenable because we hear it all the time. Often we 4 _____ its sounds filling the house, and many of us come to believe there are no others. There are. There is a long and continuing tradition of music, not only in the West but in other parts of the world, dating back hundreds of years, music that is still being played. There are operas, 5 _____ for a limited number of instruments, symphonies, concertos for orchestra and solo instruments, music to accompany ballets, and music created from non-Western scales.

6. What kind of music do many of us listen to according to the speaker? Why?
7. What types of music does the speaker mention in his talk? Make a list.
8. How does the speaker persuade a listener to be a more experienced or a wiser one?
9. What does the example of the Beatles in 1960s imply in the talk?

Section 2 Watching

Directions: Please watch the video clip and discuss the following questions in pairs or groups.

Arches in Music and Architecture

1. Have you been to a Catholic church or a Buddhist temple before? If yes, what kind of music was played there?
2. How do you think music helps religious believers during worship services?
3. What was the complex musical language Palestrina had used in his time? What does the term mean?
4. Are music and architecture in some way related to each other? How did Christophers explain the relationship between church music, worship services and religious architecture?

Part Two Reading and Writing

Pre-Reading Questions

1. Name some concert performances that you have been to.
2. Was any of them first-time performance?

Text A

Why Premieres?[1]
Thomas Forrest Kelly[2]

1   Why choose *premieres*? Why not examine, say, the last performance of a piece during the composer's lifetime or a performance of exceptional importance, either with the composer present or at some later time? After all, music is not painting; a first performance is not the "original," and the ones that follow mere copies. Later performances of a given piece, when audiences and performers have had time to reflect on its novelty and assimilate its difficulties, might in some ways be better.

2   Premieres are exciting: they are *visceral* and new. Our own experience of premieres (usually a new production of an old piece) is frequently full of anticipation and doubt. How will it go? Will the double basses[3] manage the big solo? Will the *sopranos* sing flat? Will the audience like it? We now use the word premiere as a verb: premiering is the act of bringing something into existence by performing it. This is not an operation limited to musicians, however: it is society in action, bringing into being a new cultural object. The premieres in this book required the participation of a great many people beyond musicians and listeners: writers, censors, instrument makers, floor sweepers, police, chair bearers, prostitutes, milliners, and others who were part of the scene.

3   Composers—even great composers writing great works—create for people. Aware of a given society's values and behaviors, they calculate the place of their new composition in its world. How do those involved—the composers, performers, listeners—expect it to sound? Does it sound that way when it's played? And why or why not?

4   Each great work has its infancy, when it is new and fresh, when tradition, admiration, and history have not yet affected its shape, when its audience is unencumbered by previous expectations. Its birth is a moment of importance and excitement; its creation is in performance. This is not to belittle the work of the composer, who, well before the performance, "creates" the work, or the directions for it, on paper. But surely it becomes music only when it is heard.

5   There is no particular reason that we should privilege these premieres, except perhaps to indulge our own time-travel fantasies. After all, it is our own appreciation

that we want to deepen, not that of some long-dead Mantuan[4]. The modern revival of older music, with its attempt to re-create antique performing styles and techniques—a phenomenon often associated with the terms "Early Music," "authenticity," or "historical performance"—is unique to our century. Some would call it a reflection of our own *fin-de-siècle*[5] nostalgia or restlessness. But even though our interest in a wide range of music makes a book like this a reflection of our culture, this volume is not meant as *a rallying cry* for historical purity.

It's unlikely, in fact, that we would get much musical enjoyment from one of these first performances—excitement, yes, because of our historical interest, but not deep musical pleasure. Some were probably dreadful: under-rehearsed, poorly understood, and distracting because of an *unruly* audience; they may not have represented the composer's last, or best, versions of the piece; and the performance style may have been different enough from what we are used to, or what we prefer, to make them *grotesque* to modern ears. Our interest here is in how they were heard at the time.

I am not suggesting that we ought to reconstruct first performances. Even if we could recover enough information to feel confident about details, the idea itself is problematic. First of all, the performances would probably not be considered "good"—that is, mature, well digested, well rehearsed, precise, and fully expressive. But even if they were, the act of trying to reproduce them would instantly betray us: rather than performing, we would simply be *going through somebody else's motions*.

I do believe, however, that some of the best and most exciting musical performances being given today are by performers using old techniques and *period* instruments. Musicians must somehow make the music and the performance their own—they must add to, not subtract from, a musical text.

I offer some history of performance in this book—background on the performers' technical abilities, their behavior, their instruments, their training, their place in society, their attitude toward music. Is it possible that the amazing D-flat major scale[6] played by the fourth horn near the end of the slow movement of the Nine Symphony was actually intended to be played on a hand horn with no *valves*? The curious dark color of the many notes that must be stopped with the hand in the bell of the instrument would certainly increase the sense of tonal distance[7]. Is it possible that in the double fugue[8] of "Seid unschlungen, Millionen"[9] Beethoven was not just bowing to necessity when he had the trumpets double the voice but skip certain notes—notes that the trumpet cannot play? Just possibly, the cross-rhythms this produced were helpful in the larger rhythmic profile of a complicated passage. After all, it would have been possible to leave the trumpets out entirely. These may be small details, but they just might make us think that performers and composers have often made beauty out of the materials and techniques at hand.

Although this is not a book about performance practice as such, I do reassess the ideas of unchanging performance standards. I treat every piece of music as an element of its culture, providing classic case studies. This, I hope, will help demonstrate how changing traditions of performance are important to the sound and the effect of music and possibly make an argument for the ultimate impossibility of "authentic performance."

11 As important as the study of historical performing techniques is the understanding of historical listening. Instrumental and vocal practices vary with time and place, but so do performance situations, the values placed on music and musicians, the relative importance of novelty and tradition, and the experience that a listener brings to a new piece of music. The listeners who experienced these five pieces did so with ears accustomed to music of their own time. A courtier in Mantua in 1607, familiar with *madrigals*, solo songs, and instrumental dances, might feel a special joy in seeing how a play cast in the well-known shape of a Greek theater piece uses familiar and unfamiliar musical styles to heighten and color the drama and bring the humanistic poetry to life in a spectacularly modern fashion. That listener would be struck by the novelty of melding classical mythology, modern poetry, and the sometimes daring music of Monteverdi. Those attributes, however, may not be what strikes the modern listener first.

12 Each place and time has its particular fashions and conventions, and a listener hearing a new piece fits it into a matrix of existing traditions, experiences, and *repertories*. Our own traditions, backlogs, and repertories are vastly different from those of the people who heard these pieces when they were new. An attempt to hear them as they were heard then provides each piece with a new and fresh look and sound.

13 Successive performances add to the history, the understanding, and the *baggage* of a piece. The later history of a piece, the *Rezeptionsgeschichte*[10], as some musicologists like to call it, is a study of its own: it involves a *retrospective* look at the *reciprocal effect* of a work of art on its surroundings and the progress (or lack of it) with which the work is received, understood, transmitted, described, admired, or ridiculed over time. This is essential to cultural history, to the understanding of works of art as essential and formative parts of the web of human achievement.

14 It becomes ever more clear, through the study of reception history, that the work changes: not only the perception of the work—what successive generations, or nations, think about it—but in a sense the work itself. This is especially evident, of course, for an artwork that requires performance in order to exist. In the case of an enduring musical work, like those in this book, the piece has had every opportunity to change as it travels, through modifications in instruments, patterns of rehearsal, orchestral seating, buildings and their arrangements, and ideas about how music ought to be performed to be beautiful. Only the modern recording media have frozen some of the dynamics of performance, though our varying perceptions of the same recording prove that not even the record has killed performance: perhaps it has only stunned it.

5   But here we are concerned not with the growth, only with the birth. When these pieces were new, there were no *canonical* standards for the pieces, no customary tempos, no famous conductor who took the slow *movement* a little too fast. This is the only performance the piece has ever had, and it is happening now.

(1470 words)

New Words

premiere	[prɪˈmɪə]	*n.*	the first public performance of a play or movie 初次公演
visceral	[ˈvɪsərəl]	*adj.*	obtained through intuition rather than from reasoning or observation 发自肺腑的
soprano	[səˈprɑːnəʊ]	*n.*	the highest female voice 女高音
unruly	[ˌʌnˈruːli]	*adj.*	noisy and lacking in restraint or discipline 不守规矩的
grotesque	[grə(ʊ)ˈtesk]	*adj.*	unnatural, unpleasant, and exaggerated that it upsets or shocks you 荒唐的
period	[ˈpɪərɪəd]	*adj.*	having a style typical of a particular time in history 具有某个时代特征的
valve	[vælv]	*n.*	part of a musical instrument such as a trumpet that changes the sound by controlling the flow of air (管乐器上的)活瓣
madrigal	[ˈmædrɪɡəl]	*n.*	a song sung by several singers without any musical instruments. Madrigals were popular in England in the sixteenth century. (无乐器伴奏的)合唱曲
repertory	[ˈrepət(ə)rɪ]	*n.*	a collection of works (plays, songs, operas, ballets) that an artist or company can perform and do perform for short intervals on a regular schedule 全部剧目
baggage	[ˈbæɡɪdʒ]	*n.*	the beliefs and attitudes that someone has as a result of their past experiences (因阅历而形成的)信仰、看法
retrospective	[ˌretrəʊˈspektɪv]	*adj.*	concerned with or related to the past 回顾的
canonical	[kəˈnɒnɪkəl]	*adj.*	be accepted as having all the qualities that a thing of its kind should have 标准的;典范的
movement	[ˈmuːvmənt]	*n.*	a major self-contained part of a symphony or sonata 乐章

 New Expressions

a rallying cry for	a slogan used to rally support for a cause 战斗口号
go through the motions	pretend to do something by acting as if one was really doing it 敷衍了事
reciprocal effect	an effect that bears on or binding each of two parties equally 交互影响

 **Notes**

1. The text was extracted from Introduction of the book *First Nights*, published in 2000, by Yale University. This book is about the first performances of five famous pieces of music: Monteverdi's *Orfeo* (1607), Handel's *Messiah* (1741), Beethoven's *Ninth Symphony* (1824), Berlioz's *Symphonie fantasktique* (1830), and Stravinsky's *The Rite of Spring* (1913). Each chapter focuses on one piece and presents a narrative about the preparation and execution of a single performance on a single day.

   Monteverdi, Claudio (1567—1643): Italian composer. His important works include *Orfeo* (1607) and his sacred *Vespers* (1610).

   Handel, George Frederick (1685—1759): a prolific British baroque composer (born in Germany), remembered best for his oratorio Messiah's *Messiah* (1741).

   Beethoven, Ludwig van (1770—1827): German composer of instrumental music (especially symphonic and chamber music); continued to compose after he lost his hearing. "The Nine Symphony" in the text refers to his *Ninth Symphony* (1824).

   Berlioz, Hector (1803—1869): French composer of romantic works. *Symphonie fantasktique* (1830) was one of his notable works.

   Stravinsky, Igor (1882—1971): composer who was born in Russia but lived in the United States after 1939. He made his name with the ballets *The Firebird* (1910) and *The Rite of Spring* (1913).

2. Thomas Forrest Kelly is professor of music at Harvard University. He has served as president of Early Music America, as a regular commentator for National Public Radio, and as a columnist for the magazine *Early Music Magazine*.

3. double bass: 音乐术语，即低音提琴。

4. Mantuan: people who live in Mantua, a town in Lombardy, northern Italy.

5. fin-de-siècle, 法语, end of the century.

6. D-flat major scale: 音乐术语，指降D大调音阶。

7. the sense of tonal distance: 音程感。

8. double fugue: 音乐术语，即双主题赋格曲。

9. Seid unschlungen, Millionen: 德语，意为"百万民众，拥抱在一起吧！"，源自德国诗人席勒作词、贝多芬作曲的《欢乐颂》。

10. Rezeptionsgeschichte: 德语，意为接受史，即音乐作品被后世大众接受的过程。

Task 1 Generating the Outline

Directions: Please identify the thesis of the passage and the main point of each paragraph, and then find out how these points develop the thesis.

_____

_____

_____

Task 2 Understanding the Text

Directions: Please answer the following questions based on Text A.

1. What makes an original painting different from a first time musical performance according to the author?
2. Why did the author think the premieres of the five masterpieces are "exciting"?
3. What makes a musical work music according to the author?
4. Why did the author think "it's unlikely, in fact, that we would get much musical enjoyment from one of these first performances"?
5. What is the study of reception history of a piece? In what ways is it important?
6. How did the author explain that his interest in the five premieres "is in how they were heard at the time"?

Task 3 Learning the Words and Phrases

Directions: Please fill in the blanks in the sentences below with the words or phrases listed in the box. Change the forms if necessary.

> premiere   a rallying cry   soprano   repertory   go through the motions

1. You can take a personal journey, like starting a socially conscious business, and turn it into _____ for an army of aspiring entrepreneurs.
2. She possesses a _____ voice of unusually fine quality.
3. Hepburn attends a benefit _____ of "Roman Holiday", the movie that made her a superstar, in 1953.
4. If you're going to _____ every day, putting minimal effort into the job you say you hate, you will definitely not feel fulfilled.
5. I restage dances from the classical _____, document old dances, and pass on the tradition to the next generation.

Task 4 Translating the Sentences

Directions: Please translate the following sentences into Chinese.

1. Composers—even great composers writing great works—create for people. Aware of a given society's values and behaviors, they calculate the place of their new composition in its world.

2. There is no particular reason that we should privilege these premieres, except perhaps to indulge our own time-travel fantasies.

3. It's unlikely, in fact, that we would get much musical enjoyment from one of these first performances—excitement, yes, because of our historical interest, but not deep musical pleasure.

4. Instrumental and vocal practices vary with time and place, but so do performance situations, the values placed on music and musicians, the relative importance of novelty and tradition, and the experience that a listener brings to a new piece of music.

5. In the case of an enduring musical work, like those in this book, the piece has had every opportunity to change as it travels, through modifications in instruments, patterns of rehearsal, orchestral seating, buildings and their arrangements, and ideas about how music ought to be performed to be beautiful.

Task 5 Writing Exercises

Directions: Please answer the following questions according to your understanding of the text.

1. Choose one paragraph from the text. Discuss with your classmate what transitions (connectors) the author used to keep a good coherence and unity in it.

2. Do you think that the text has a perfect unity? Why do you think that way? Are there any sentences in any paragraphs that are off-topic, i.e. sentences that don't have anything to do with the major goals of the writing?

Unit 4

Directions: Write a personal response in 300 words to one of the issues discussed in the text, using at least six commonly used transitions to maintain a good unity. Be sure to write a topic sentence that helps the reader anticipate the organization of your written work.

Part Three   Reading and Speaking

Pre-Reading Questions

1. Do you listen to music? What do you listen for?
2. Name as many types of music as you can. Discuss with your friend what makes them different from each other.

Text B

Music and the Social World[1]
Jeanette Bicknell[2]

1   Here is the task at hand: explain why music is generally valued and moving to many people as a preliminary to making sense of the particular issue of why some music is extremely, even profoundly, moving. To do this, one of the central things we need to come to terms with is the idea that music and the experience of music are fundamentally social, rather than strictly personal or individual. But what exactly does this claim mean, and what implications might be drawn from it? The philosopher Ludwig Wittgenstein[3] is well known for (among other things) his "private language argument," undercutting the idea that the meanings of the terms in a language might be known only by a single user. *In a similar vein*, yet without actually applying his argument to music, I hope to show that there could be no strictly private musical experience.

2   Human beings are social animals. Plato and Aristotle, among the earliest in the western tradition to address the peculiar nature of humankind, reject the idea that a human being could exist apart from a social order. Aristotle famously remarked that anyone living outside of a community would be "either subhuman or superhuman." A growing number of researchers provide an evolutionary perspective on these ancient

philosophical speculations. They suggest that *hominid* brain expansion was driven largely by social factors. For example, face-to-face interaction places demands on working memory and may have been an influence on frontal lobe development. Furthermore, the grasp of symbolic relationships which makes language possible (and indeed language itself) could have proceeded from the need to manage the complexities of increasingly large social groups.

3   The recognition of music as a human (rather than a natural or supernatural) product goes hand-in-hand with its fundamentally social character. This can be seen in many ways. Music is created (composed, *improvised*, performed) by human beings, usually for the benefit of other human beings. Even in those cultures where *unmediated* natural sound can be considered music (and there are only very few of these), the grouping of natural sound with song or instrumental music is a social convention. The transmission of music from one generation to the next begins very early in life. Think of the universal practice of singing children to sleep, and the existence everywhere of a special musical repertory for children. Musical culture relies on human transmission. If a group were to disappear and leave behind no comprehensible record of its music-making, we would have no idea what its musical culture was like. Even musicians who are self-taught must rely on other human beings (or recordings of them) to grasp how their instruments are supposed to sound, not to mention how to make sounds into a musical work.

4   So far the connections I have noted between music and the social character should be uncontroversial. Yet there are additional ways in which music is dependent on the social world and social realities. Most crucially, systems of musical meaning are conventional; that is, they rely on human agreement in a number of crucial ways. First, what counts as music in each society rests on cultural agreement. Random sounds are not music. Even in the case of *avant-garde* music that employs random sounds, human design or intention must enter at some stage. All societies place limits on music-making, such that certain sounds are accepted as musical while others are excluded. Human beings make music only in particular ways. The range of variety present in the world's musical cultures is considerably narrower than the scope of imaginable sound patterns. Similarly, the underlying patterns which give music meaning are also conventional. One cannot make music out of nothing. Musical resources—many musical instruments and some of their performance practices, the capacities of the human voice, rhythmic and tonal patterns—pre-exist individual musicians and composers. This is the case even as composers sometimes invent new musical instruments and challenge the capacities of the human voice. Different musical cultures are based on different patterns of tonal and rhythmic organization. Understanding the music of an unfamiliar culture requires familiarity with these underlying patterns, usually acquired through guided listening. These patterns of musical structure and meaning are social constructions which evolved through human musical practice. Composers who challenge the limits of their sub-culture's

musical conventions must presuppose and engage with those conventions in order for their music to sound novel. Furthermore, by the time an individual's sound productions are considered music (even inferior music) rather than noise or mere sound, he will already have begun to assimilate the patterns of musical organization specific to his culture. A child's random banging on pots and pans is usually considered noise rather than music. However, if he sings a recognizable but out-of-tune melody, this has at least some claim to the status of music-making.

I should say here that just because a practice is conventional that does not *entail* that it is necessarily arbitrary. The original association between a red traffic light and the obligation to stop is arbitrary; however, once established, particular conventions may be followed for reasons of convenience or *expediency*. It makes sense for different *jurisdictions* to share the same traffic signal conventions to some extent. Still other conventions may have a basis in the nature of things. For example, the convention about the zero of the Kelvin[4] temperature scale is backed by the *postulate* that there is no molecular activity below 0° K. So the claim that systems of music meaning are conventional does not entail the very different claim that they are wholly arbitrary. Indeed, they are probably not. The fact that we can come to understand the music of different cultures probably indicates that such systems have a natural basis in human auditory processing capacities. (Indeed, this is suggested by a great deal of research in both psychology and *ethnomusicology*.)

Now, some readers will think that I have stressed the obvious. Others may find my characterization of musical experience as fundamentally social to be *counterintuitive*. Before continuing it seems a good idea to address some objections to the account just laid out.

(1012 words)

New Words

hominid	[ˈhɒmɪnɪd]	*adj.*	relating to, or belonging to the Hominidae 人科的;和人科有关的
improvise	[ˈɪmprəvaɪz]	*v.*	make or do something using whatever you have or without having planned it in advance 即兴创作;临时提供
unmediated	[ʌnˈmiːdieɪtɪd]	*adj.*	having no intervening persons, agents, conditions 未调停的
avant-garde	[ˌævɒŋˈɡɑːd]	*adj.*	modern and experimental 前卫的
entail	[ɪnˈteɪl]	*v.*	involve something or cause something 牵连;导致
expediency	[ɪkˈspiːdiənsi;-əns]	*n.*	doing what is convenient rather than what is morally right 权宜之计

jurisdiction	[ˌdʒʊərɪsˈdɪkʃən]	n.	the territory within which power can be exercised 行政辖区
postulate	[ˈpɒstjʊleɪt]	n.	a proposition that is accepted as true in order to provide a basis for 假定,假设
ethnomusicology	[ˈeθnəʊˌmjuːzɪˈkɒlədʒɪ]		an academic field encompassing various approaches to the study of music (broadly defined) that emphasizes its cultural, social, material, cognitive, biological, and other dimensions or contexts instead of or in addition to its isolated sound component or any particular repertoire 人种音乐学,民族音乐学
counterintuitive	[ˌkaʊntərɪnˈtjuːɪtɪv]	adj.	contrary to what common sense would suggest 反直观的,反直觉的

New Expressions

in a similar vein	in a similar style or manner 以类似的方式或风格

Notes

1. The text is extracted from *Why Music Moves Us*, written by Jeanette Bicknell, and published by Palgrave Macmillan in 2009. The book mainly focuses on issues like "why music has the power to move us" and "why does it have this effect on us? What is going on, emotionally, physically and cognitively when listeners have strong emotional responses to music? What, if anything, do such responses mean? Can they tell us anything about ourselves?"
2. Jeanette Bicknell teaches philosophy in Ottawa, Canada. She has written widely on aesthetics and philosophy of music.
3. Ludwig Wittgenstein (1889—1951): British philosopher born in Austria; a major influence on logic and logical positivism.
4. The Kelvin temperature scale has absolute zero as its zero point, and its fundamental unit is the kelvin. 克尔文温标以绝对零度为其零点,基本单位是克尔文。

Task 1 Questions for Comprehension

Directions: Please answer the following questions based on Text B.

1. What was the claim the author made in the first paragraph? What does it mean?
2. What does Aristotle mean by "either subhuman or superhuman"?
3. How did the ancient philosophical speculations prove right according to the author?
4. What were the connections the author made between music and its social character?

5. How did the author develop her argument that different musical systems share "a natural basis in human auditory processing capacities"?

Task 2　Questions for Discussion

Directions: Discuss the following questions in pairs or groups.

1. Name one piece of your favorite songs and explain why you like it.
2. The author believed that music and the experience of music are fundamentally social, rather than strictly personal and individual. How would you respond to it? Take your position and use your personal experience to illustrate your points.
3. Some people believe that "music and the experience of music are personal or individual." Could you please help come up with some possible reasons for the statement? What makes them think that way?
4. Make a three-minute non-stop speech on Music and the Social World. You may just retell the key points discussed in the text or develop your ideas on any of the issues discussed.

Part Four　Cross Cultural Communication

Passage A

中国古代音乐的文化内涵[1]

靳婕[2]

　　中国传统文化植根于农耕文明，十分重视自然的和谐统一，即人与自然、人与社会的和谐，人与人之间以及人的身心和谐。中国古代哲学的主流思想认为，人的自然生命与宇宙万物的生命是协调、统一的，即"天人合一"。这一观念最早出自名家惠施的"泛爱万物，天地一体也"，意思是说，人类应当不分贵贱地善待自然万物，因为两者本质上是相通的。

　　"天人合一"也是中国古代先贤们追求的最高音乐境界。追根溯源，中国音乐一开始即以自然为其"第一主题"。在著名的古琴曲《高山流水》中，作曲者对巍巍高山和涓涓流水的自然景观作了模拟表现。不同于西方音乐中所描绘的山水，该曲对山水的模拟表现已把山水与人融为一体，作曲者借物寄情，寓情于山水之间。这种"山水即人，人即山水"的主题也同样体现在《春江花月夜》《渔舟唱晚》《平沙落雁》《梅花三弄》《平湖秋月》《二泉映月》等众多中国传统名曲中。人与自然在音乐中相互融合、合为一体，而非自然的旁观者、欣赏者，这正是中国古代"天人合一"的文化精神在音乐中的体现。

　　中国古代的思想家们认为，音乐与自然、人、社会相通相契，是一种具有深刻的自然和社会意义的文化，但各家学派的音乐审美寓意又有不同，如儒家孔子的礼乐思想和道家老庄的"天人合一"，都是建立在"和"，即"乐者，天地之和"的思想基础上，两者都将音乐的存在与自然、社会紧密地联系起来。道家强调顺应天性的"天乐""天籁"音乐观，即自然本色之美；儒家则在此基础上，将音乐视为调适情感、修身养性的文化手段，并认为音乐具有教化民风、考察政治得失、协调社会伦理秩序的多重作用。此外，佛家之禅宗"以心感悟"（即认为对于音乐的感受，心性是很重要的）的音乐思想，也受到许多中国传统文人的推崇。

　　古代儒、道和禅宗三家共有的"天人合一"的自然观对中国传统音乐文化影响极其深远。这种自然观认为，音乐艺术创造于物我互通、心物交感之中，"天人合一"因而成为中国古代音乐的最高审美标准。若想深入了解中国民族音乐的精髓，对中国古代音乐文化内涵的领悟和欣赏是必不可少的。

(906字)

1. 本文选自靳婕编著：《中国音乐》，五洲传播出版社，2010年。
2. 编著者靳婕，女，毕业于中国音乐学院音乐学系，中国音乐家协会世界民族音乐学会会员。著有《指挥大师与作品演奏：名指挥·名乐团·名唱片》等。

Task 1　Questions for Comprehension and Discussion

Directions: Please answer the following questions.

1. Name the five well-known musical works mentioned in the article.
2. Discuss the common characters in the titles of the well-known musical works.
3. What are the main Chinese traditional thoughts introduced in the passage?

Task 2　Summary

Directions: You are invited to give a talk in English on How Traditional Chinese Culture Has a Profound Impact on Ancient Music of China. The audience are mainly international students on campus. Write a report in 300 words summarizing the main ideas of the passage for the talk.

Passage B

The Musical Legacies of Antiquity[1]

Mark Evan Bonds[2]

　　Although the music of antiquity was essentially lost to the medieval era, the attitudes of the ancient Greeks and Romans toward music have exerted an unbroken influence on Western thinking about the art down to the present day. Many of these attitudes and beliefs found their expression in myth. Other aspects of ancient perspectives toward music can be gleaned from philosophy, drama, poetry, and through writings concerned directly with music itself.

Music and the Cosmos

　　Pythagoras (6th century B. C. E) is credited with having discovered the relationship between musical sound and number. According to legend, Pythagoras was passing by a blacksmith's forge one day and noticed that hammers of different weights were creating sounds in the intervals of an octave, a fifth, and a fourth. When he weighed the hammers, he discovered that their weight fell into the ratio 2:1 (octave), 3:2 (fifth), and 4:3 (fourth). Because of their mathematical simplicity, these intervals were considered "perfect" consonances. Pythagoras considered the mathematical basis of sound a fundamental law governing the relationship of all physical bodies in the universe.

Music and the Soul

The same forces perceived to govern the cosmos, including music, were also understood by the ancients to govern the human soul. Music thus had the power to alter behavior in the most fundamental way, creating either harmony or discord within the spirit of the individual.

The myth of Orpheus and Euridice gives powerful expression to this belief. Orpheus was a celebrated musician capable of calming wild beasts with his playing. When his wife, Euridice, died on their wedding day, he attempted to retrieve her from the underworld, Hades. To do so, he had to persuade the guardians of Hades to allow him—a mortal—to cross into the realm of the dead and then return to life. Charon, the boatman who ferries dead souls across the River Styx, refused this absurd request, but Orpheus' skill on the lyre was so powerful that Charon was overwhelmed and fell into a deep sleep. Orpheus similarly used music to persuade Pluto, god of the underworld, to release Euridice. The story thus suggests that through music, humans can bridge the otherwise unbridgeable divide between life and death.

Like the god Pluto, even the most powerful mortals are helpless to resist the spell of music. Not even the great Odysseus could resist the Sirens, whose seductive song lured sailors to dash their boats to pieces on their rock. The goddess Circe warned Odysseus that he could safely pass the Sirens only by plugging the ears of his crew with thick wax. Odysseus permitted himself to hear the Sirens' song after commanding his men to bind him to the mast of his ship.

The belief that music has the power to elevate or debase the soul, to enlighten or degrade the mind, was widespread in antiquity and is still current today. The doctrine of ethos held that music was capable of arousing listeners to certain kinds of emotions and behaviors. Plato, in the late 4th century B.C.E., recommended that youths learn to make music in the Dorian and Phrygian modes: for former because it imparted courage, the latter because it imparted thoughtfulness. Aristotle observed that some modes "make men noticeably mournful and restrained in mood, like the so-called Mixolydian," whereas other modes "soften the temper of the active intelligence.... It is the same with rhythms: some have a remarkably stable ethos, others an ethos which stirs the emotions; and of this latter class some are notably vulgar in their emotional effects while others better suit freeborn persons."

Music and the State

The same powers that affect the individual also affect the state—which is, after all, a collection of individuals. Music education was thus an element of good citizenship in ancient Greece, for youth of both sexes. "Music has the power of producing a certain effect on the moral character of the soul," Aristotle declared, "and if it has the power to do this, it is clear that the young must be directed to music and must be educated in it." His teacher Plato had taken a far more restrictive approach to music education, even while acknowledging its importance:

The overseers of our state must... be watchful against innovations in music and gymnastics counter to the established order, and to the best of their power guard against them.... For a change to a new type music is something to beware of as a hazard of all our fortunes. For the modes of music are never disturbed without unsettling of the most fundamental political and social conventions.

This fear of the subversive power of unfamiliar music (or any music) has cropped up countless times over the centuries. In the 20th century alone, older generations have condemned ragtime (in the 1910s), jazz (1920s), rock and roll (1950s and 1960s), heavy metal (1980s), and rap (1990s) as threats to the morals of American youth. The danger was seen to reside not only in the lyrics but also in the music itself, either because of its rhythm (ragtime, jazz, rock and roll) or volume and timbre (heavy metal). In one way or another, all of these repertories created anxiety about the disruption of the established order.

Vocal versus Instrumental Music

In Greek, the word *mousike* was understood to encompass not only elements of melody and rhythm, but also the words being sung and even the dance that might accompany them. Poetry and song, in Greek culture, were virtually indistinguishable. Instrumental music was thus seen as an inherently lesser art than vocal music. It was welcomed in its place but held in lower esteem. Aristotle, for example, argued that vocal music was superior to instrumental music because voices, whether human or animal, are found only in creatures that have a soul.

At the same time, instrumental music was regarded with a certain mixture of awe and suspicion, precisely because it was able to move listeners without recourse to words. Instrumental music is so elemental that it works at a level not fully susceptible to rational explanation. This helps explain the uneasy mix of attitudes toward instrumental music—condescension mixed with an acute awareness of its powers—that would characterize Western attitudes for the next 2,000 years.

(1034 words)

 Notes

1. The text was extracted from *A Brief History of Music in Western Culture* (《西方文化中的音乐简史》), written by Mark Evan Bonds, published by Peking University Press, 2004.
2. Mark Evan Bonds is the Cary C. Boshamer Distinguished Professor of Music at the University of North Carolina at Chapel Hill, where he has taught since 1992.

Task 1 Questions for Comprehension and Discussion

Directions: Please answer the following questions.

1. According to the passage how can we still feel the influence of the music of antiquity (i.e. the ancient Greek and Roman culture) at the present day?
2. Which one of the four subheadings in the passage impresses you most? Explain why and briefly retell its main idea.

3. Work with your partner and make a comparison between the roots of Western and Chinese music.

Task 2   Summary

Directions: You have just had a talk on The Connotation of Ancient Music of China last week and now you think it is interesting to explore something about the origin of Western music. Please write a summary of The Musical Legacies of Antiquity in Chinese in 500 characters.

Unit 5

DEMOCRACY AND LAW

Our exercise of political power is fully proper only when it is exercised in accordance with a constitution the essentials of which all citizens as free and equal may reasonably be expected to endorse in the light of principles and ideals acceptable to their common human reason.

—*John Rawls*

Learning Objectives

Upon the completion of this unit, you should be able to:

Remembering & Understanding	★ master the new words in Text A and Text B; ★ understand the basic conceptions in politics, such as justice, equality, liberty, and democracy, etc.;
Analyzing & Applying	★ analyze the structure of an argument: premises and conclusion; ★ defend your position by using arguments;
Evaluating & Creating	★ evaluate an argument for its strength of reasoning; ★ write an argumentative essay; ★ develop your ideas of social justice.

Unit 5

Part One Lead-in

Section 1 Listening

Directions: Please fill in the blanks with words or sentences on the basis of what you have heard in the audio clip. Then discuss the following questions in pairs or groups.

Rawls and His Theory of Justice

Rawls is a key figure with many key ideas. So through ideas that sound really 1_____ the first time you encounter them such as the hypothetical contract, the original position, the veil of ignorance, he actually shows something very important and very simple, namely that we can argue with some precision over what impartial and 2_____ distribution would require. So we can recognise for example that we might be 3_____ in various ways. And Rawls's suggestion was what types of steps we might take to get rid of these biases when we are being asked how we should 4_____ goods in society. And of course we are familiar with the thought that we should eliminate religious, gender, racial biases. What Rawls also says is that we should eliminate 5_____ biases. So he suggests that when we face the question how to distribute goods in society we should imagine that we don't know whether we are talented. And if you don't know whether you are talented and how well you are going to fare in the market for example you might be more willing to accept that even the untalented should get jobs that are well 6_____. And even add the cost to salaries to the very talented. Why you might ask, should we eliminate talent bias? Well Rawls gives us the story mainly that much of our talent isn't actually within our control. It's a function of our family background, our class, the native talent we are born with. And so we should be wary of thinking that people who are lucky to have been born talented should therefore end up scooping the best prizes that market might offer.

7. What key ideas are mentioned in the conversation?
8. What biases have to be got rid of in the distribution of social goods?
9. What is the debate that Rawls revived?

Section 2 Watching

Directions: please watch the video clip and discuss the following questions in pairs or groups.

Introduction to Political Philosophy

1. What is political philosophy about?
2. How is political philosophy to be studied?

Part Two Reading and Writing

Pre-Reading Questions

1. What do you think politics is about? What do you know about political philosophy?
2. What is your understanding of justice? Please give examples to show the distinction between justice and injustice.
3. Could you say something about political rights, and social or economic equalities/inequalities?

Text A

Two Principles of Justice[1]
John Rawls[2]

1 I shall now state in a provisional form the two principles of *justice* that I believe would be chosen in the original position. The first formulation of these principles is tentative. As we *go on* I shall consider several formulations and approximate *step by step* the final statement to be given much later. I believe that doing this allows the exposition to proceed in a natural way.

　　First: each person is to have an equal right to the most extensive basic liberty compatible with a similar *liberty* for others.

　　Second: social and economic inequalities are to be arranged so that they are both (a) reasonably expected to be to everyone's advantage, and (b) attached to positions and offices open to all.

2 *By way of* general comment, these principles primarily *apply*, as I have said, *to* the basic structure of society. They are to govern the assignment of rights and duties and to regulate the distribution of social and economic advantages. As their formulation suggests, these principles presuppose that the social structure can be divided into two more or less distinct parts, the first principle applying to the one, the second to the other. They distinguish between those aspects of the social system that define and *secure* the equal liberties of *citizenship* and those that specify and establish social and economic inequalities. The basic liberties of citizens are, roughly speaking, political liberty (the right to vote and to *be eligible for* public office) together with freedom of speech and *assembly*; liberty of *conscience* and freedom of thought; freedom of the person along with the right to hold (personal) property; and freedom from arbitrary arrest and seizure as defined by the concept of the rule of law. These liberties are all required to be equal by the first principle, since citizens of a just society are to have the same basic rights.

3 The second principle applies, in the first *approximation*, to the distribution of income and wealth and to the design of organizations that make use of differences in

authority and responsibility, or chains of command. While the distribution of wealth and income need not be equal, it must be to everyone's advantage, and at the same time, positions of authority and offices of command must be accessible to all. One applies the second principle by holding positions open, and then, subject to this constraint, arranges social and economic inequalities so that everyone benefits.

These principles are to be arranged in a serial order with the first principle *prior to* the second. This ordering means that a departure from the institutions of equal liberty required by the first principle cannot be *justified* by, or *compensated* for, by greater social and economic advantages. The distribution of wealth and income, and the *hierarchies* of authority, must be consistent with both the liberties of equal citizenship and equality of opportunity.

It is clear that these principles are rather specific in their content, and their acceptance rests on certain assumptions that I must eventually try to explain and justify. A theory of justice depends upon a theory of society in ways that will become evident as we proceed. For the present, it should be observed that the two principles (and this holds for all formulations) are a special case of a more general conception of justice that can be expressed as follows.

> All social values—liberty and opportunity, income and wealth, and the bases of self-respect—are to be distributed equally unless an unequal distribution of any, or all, of these values is to everyone's advantage.

Injustice, then, is simply inequalities that are not *to the benefit of* all. Of course, this conception is extremely vague and requires interpretation.

As a first step, suppose that the basic structure of society distributes certain primary goods, that is, things that every rational man is presumed to want. These goods normally have a use whatever a person's *rational* plan of life. For simplicity, assume that the chief primary goods at the disposition of society are rights and liberties, powers and opportunities, income and wealth. These are the social primary goods. Other primary goods such as health and vigor, intelligence and imagination, are natural goods; although their possession is influenced by the basic structure, they are not so directly under its control. Imagine, then, a hypothetical initial arrangement in which all the social primary goods are equally distributed: everyone has similar rights and duties, and income and wealth are evenly shared. This state of affairs provides a *benchmark* for judging improvements. If certain inequalities of wealth and organizational powers would make everyone *better off* than in this hypothetical starting situation, then they *accord with* the general conception.

Now it is possible, at least theoretically, that by giving up some of their fundamental liberties men are sufficiently compensated by the resulting social and economic gains. The general conception of justice imposes no restrictions on what sort of inequalities are permissible; it only requires that everyone's position be improved. We need not suppose anything so drastic as *consenting* to a condition of slavery.

Imagine instead that men *forego* certain political rights when the economic returns are significant and their capacity to influence the course of policy by the exercise of these rights would be *marginal* in any case. It is this kind of exchange which the two principles as stated *rule out*; being arranged in serial order they do not permit exchanges between basic liberties and economic and social gains. The serial ordering of principles expresses an underlying preference among primary social goods. When this preference is rational so likewise is the choice of these principles in this order.

8 In developing justice as fairness I shall, for the most part, leave aside the general conception of justice and examine instead the special case of the two principles in serial order. The advantage of this procedure is that from the first the matter of priorities is recognized and an effort made to find principles to deal with it. One is led to *attend* throughout *to* the conditions under which the acknowledgment of the absolute weight of liberty *with respect to* social and economic advantages, as defined by the lexical order of the two principles, would be reasonable. *Offhand*, this ranking appears extreme and too special a case to be of much interest; but there is more justification for it than would appear *at first sight*. Furthermore, the distinction between fundamental rights and liberties and economic and social benefits marks a difference among primary social goods that one should try to exploit. It suggests an important division in the social system. Of course, the distinctions drawn and the ordering proposed *are bound to* be at best only approximations. There are surely circumstances in which they fail. But it is essential to depict clearly the main lines of a reasonable conception of justice; and under many conditions anyway, the two principles in serial order may serve well enough. When necessary we can *fall back on* the more general conception.

(1147 words)

New Words

justice	[ˈdʒʌstɪs]	*n.*	the quality of being just or fair 正义
liberty	[ˈlɪbətɪ]	*n.*	immunity from arbitrary exercise of authority; political independence 自由
secure	[sɪˈkjʊə]	*v.*	make certain of 保证
citizenship	[ˈsɪtɪzənʃɪp]	*n.*	the status of a citizen with rights and duties 公民身份
eligible	[ˈelɪdʒəbl]	*adj.*	qualified for or allowed or worthy of being chosen 合格的，有资格当选的
assembly	[əˈsemblɪ]	*n.*	a group of persons gathered together for a common purpose 集会
conscience	[ˈkɒnʃəns]	*n.*	motivation deriving logically from ethical or moral principles that govern a person's thoughts and actions 道德心，良心

Unit 5

approximation	[əˌprɒksɪˈmeɪʃən]	*n.*	an approximate calculation of quantity or degree or worth 近似
justify	[ˈdʒʌstɪfaɪ]	*v.*	show to be reasonable or provide adequate ground for 证明……是正当的
compensate	[ˈkɒmpenseɪt]	*v.*	make up for shortcomings or a feeling of inferiority by exaggerating good qualities 补偿
hierarchy	[ˈhaɪərɑːkɪ]	*n.*	a series of ordered groupings of people or things within a system 等级制度
rational	[ˈræʃənəl]	*adj.*	consistent with or based on or using reason 合理的，理性的
benchmark	[ˈbentʃmɑːk]	*n.*	a standard by which something can be measured or judged 基准
consent	[kənˈsent]	*v.*	give an affirmative reply to; respond favorably to 同意
forego	[fɔːˈgəʊ]	*v.*	go back further 放弃
marginal	[ˈmɑːdʒɪnəl]	*adj.*	of questionable or minimal quality 不重要的，少量的
offhand	[ˈɒfhænd]	*adv.*	without previous thought or preparation 未经核实地

New Expressions

go on	continue 继续下去
step by step	dealing with one thing and then another thing in a fixed order 逐步地
by way of	as a form or means of sonething 用作；作为
apply to	lend itself to 适用于
be eligible for	be qualified for 符合……的条件
prior to	ahead of 在……之前
to the benefit of	in favor of 有利于
better off	in a more fortunate or prosperous condition 状况好的
accord with	be in line with 同……相符合，与……一致
rule out	preclude 排除
attend to	pay atlention to 注意
with respect to	concerning 关于
at first sight	when first seen or considered 初看之下
be bound to	be certain to 必然，一定要
fall back on	to have something to use when you are in difficulty 求助于；转而依靠

Notes

1. The text is excerpted from Section 11 Chapter 2 of *A Theory of Justice*, originally published in 1971 and revised in both 1975 (for translated edition) and 1999.
2. John Rawls (February 21, 1921—November 24, 2002) was an American moral and political

philosopher. He held the James Bryant Conant University Professorship at Harvard University and the Fulbright Fellowship at Christ Church, Oxford. Rawls received both the Schock Prize for Logic and Philosophy and the National Humanities Medal in 1999, the latter presented by President Bill Clinton, in recognition of how Rawls's work "helped a whole generation of learned Americans revive their faith in democracy itself." His *magnum opus, A Theory of Justice* (1971), was said at the time of its publication to be "the most important work in moral philosophy since the end of World War II" and is now regarded as "one of the primary texts in political philosophy". His work in political philosophy, dubbed Rawlsianism, takes as its starting point the argument that "the most reasonable principles of justice are those everyone would accept and agree to from a fair position." Rawls attempts to determine the principles of social justice by employing a number of thought experiments such as the famous original position in which everyone is impartially situated as equals behind a veil of ignorance. He is one of the major thinkers in the tradition of liberal political philosophy. According to English philosopher Jonathan Wolff, while there could be a "dispute about the second most important political philosopher of the 20th century, there could be no dispute about the most important: John Rawls."

Task 1 Generating the Outline

Directions: Please identify the thesis of the passage and the main point of each paragraph, and then find out how these points develop the thesis.

_____
_____
_____
_____
_____
_____
_____
_____

Task 2 Understanding the Text

Directions: Please answer the following questions based on Text A.

1. What are the two principles of justice presented by Rawls?
2. What are the two different aspects of the social system that the two principles distinguish?
3. What are the basic liberties of citizens? Why are they all required to be equal by the first principle?
4. What are the two important points concerning the application of the second principle?
5. What does it imply that the two principles are arranged in a serial order?
6. What is the general conception of justice embodied in the two principles?
7. What can be inferred from the general conception of justice regarding the notion of injustice?
8. Could you give examples to show the distinction between social goods and natural goods?

Unit 5

9. What kind of function can Rawls' hypothetical initial arrangement serve?
10. What kind of exchange do the two principles rule out? Why?
11. What, according to Rawls, is the advantage of leaving aside the general conception of justice in developing justice as fairness?
12. What does the distinction between fundamental rights and liberties and economic and social benefits suggest?

Task 3 Learning the Phrases

Directions: Please fill in the blanks in the sentences blow with the phrases listed in the box. Change the forms if necessary.

> compatible with   apply to   eligible for   subject to   rule out

1. These regulations _____ everyone, without exception.
2. If your hair is thinning, it may be best to check with your doctor to _____ illness as a cause of unhealthy hair.
3. On the plus side, you may be _____ part-time unemployment benefits, depending on your state's laws, which can cushion the blow while you look for a new full-time position.
4. Johnson Moving and Storage enables employees to work remotely when that is _____ their job.
5. Foreign workers are _____ background checks before being allowed into the _____ country.

Task 4 Translating the Sentences

Directions: Please translate the following sentences into Chinese.

1. The basic liberties of citizens are, roughly speaking, political liberty (the right to vote and to be eligible for public office) together with freedom of speech and assembly; liberty of conscience and freedom of thought; freedom of the person along with the right to hold (personal) property; and freedom from arbitrary arrest and seizure as defined by the concept of the rule of law.

2. While the distribution of wealth and income need not be equal, it must be to everyone's advantage, and at the same time, positions of authority and offices of command must be accessible to all.

3. The distribution of wealth and income, and the hierarchies of authority, must be consistent with both the liberties of equal citizenship and equality of opportunity.

4. All social values—liberty and opportunity, income and wealth, and the bases of self-respect—are to be distributed equally unless an unequal distribution of any, or all, of these values is to everyone's advantage.

___

5. Imagine, then, a hypothetical initial arrangement in which all the social primary goods are equally distributed: everyone has similar rights and duties, and income and wealth are evenly shared.

___

Task 5   Writing Exercises

Directions: Write an essay reviewing Rawls' conception of justice.

___

Directions: Giving talented people rewards that would provide them with an incentive for exercising their talents is good for us all, since they are presumably productive and thereby add to the common wealth. Is this policy compatible with Rawls' conception of justice? Write an essay discussing this issue.

___

Part Three   Reading and Speaking

Pre-Reading Questions
1. How do you understand equality in politics?
2. Could you say something about liberty?
3. What do you think about the relationship between equality and liberty?

Unit 5

Text B

Equality, Liberty and Democracy
Ronald Dworkin

Equality

1   No government is legitimate unless it *subscribes to* two *reigning* principles. First, it must show equal concern for the fate of every person over whom it claims *dominion*. Second, it must respect fully the responsibility and right of each person to decide for himself how to make something valuable of his life. These guiding principles place boundaries around acceptable theories of distributive justice—theories that stipulate the resources and opportunities a government should make available to people it governs. I put the matter that way, *in terms of* what governments should do, because any distribution is the consequence of official law and policy: there is no politically neutral distribution. Given any combination of personal qualities of talent, personality, and luck, what a person will have by way of resource and opportunity will depend on the laws in place where he is governed. So every distribution must be justified by showing how what government has done respects these two fundamental principles of equal concern for fate and full respect for responsibility.

2   A *laissez-faire* political economy leaves unchanged the consequences of a free market in which people buy and sell their product and labor as they wish and can. That does not show equal concern for everyone. Anyone *impoverished* through that system *is entitled to* ask: "There are other, more *regulatory* and redistributive, sets of laws that would put me in a better position. How can government claim that this system shows equal concern for me?" It is no answer that people must take responsibility for their own fate. People are not responsible for much of what determines their place in such an economy. They are not responsible for their genetic *endowment* and innate talent. They are not responsible for the good and bad luck they have throughout their lives. There is nothing in the second principle, about personal responsibility, that would entitle government to adopt such a *posture*.

3   Suppose government makes the extreme opposite choice, however: to make wealth equal no matter what choices people made for themselves. Every few years, as would be possible in a Monopoly game, government calls in everyone's wealth and redistributes it in equal shares. That would fail to respect people's responsibility to make something of their own lives, because what people chose to do—their choices about work or recreation and about saving or investment—would then have no personal consequences. People are not responsible unless they make choices *with an eye to* the costs to others of the choices that they make. If I spend my life at leisure, or work at a job that does not produce as much as I could of what other people need or want, then I should take responsibility for the cost this choice imposes: I should have less *in consequence*.

4   The question of distributive justice therefore *calls for* a solution to simultaneous equations. We must try to find a solution that respects both the reigning principles of equal concern and personal responsibility, and we must try to do this in a way that compromises neither principle but rather finds attractive conceptions of each that fully satisfy both. Here is a fanciful illustration of a solution. Imagine an initial *auction* of all available resources in which everyone starts with the same number of bidding chips. The auction lasts a very long time, and will be repeated as long as anyone wishes. It must end in a situation in which nobody envies anybody else's bundle of resources; for that reason the distribution of resources that results treats everyone with equal concern. Then imagine a further auction in which these people design and choose comprehensive insurance policies, paying the premium the market establishes for the coverage each chooses. That auction does not eliminate the consequences of good or bad luck, but it makes people responsible for their own risk management.

Liberty

5   Justice requires a theory of liberty as well as a theory of resource equality, and we must be aware, in constructing that theory, of the danger that liberty and equality will conflict. It was Isaiah Berlin's claim that such conflict is inevitable. I argue for a theory of liberty that eliminates that danger. I distinguish your freedom, which is simply your ability to do anything you might want to do without government constraint, from your liberty, which is that part of your freedom that government would do wrong to constrain. I do not *endorse* any general right to freedom. I argue, instead, for rights to liberty that rest on different bases. People have a right to ethical independence that follows from the principle of personal responsibility. They have rights, including rights to free speech, that are required by their more general right to govern themselves, which right also flows from personal responsibility. They have rights, including rights to due process of law and freedom of property, that follow from their right to equal concern.

6   This scheme for liberty rules out genuine conflict with the conception of equality just described because the two conceptions are thoroughly integrated: each depends on the same solution to the simultaneous equation problem. You cannot determine what liberty requires without also deciding what distribution of property and opportunity shows equal concern for all. The popular view that *taxation* invades liberty is false *on this account* provided that what government takes from you can be justified *on* moral *grounds* so that it does not take from you what you are entitled to retain. A theory of liberty is in that way embedded in a much more general political morality and draws from the other parts of that theory. The alleged conflict between liberty and equality disappears.

Democracy

7   But there is another supposed conflict among our political values. This is the

conflict between equality and liberty, on the one hand, and the right to participate as an equal in one's own governance, on the other. Political theorists sometimes call the latter a right to positive liberty and suppose that that right may conflict with negative liberty—the rights to freedom from government I just described—and also with the right to a just distribution of resources. The conflict is realized, *on this view*, when a majority votes for an unjust tax scheme or a denial of important liberties. I respond to that claim of conflict by distinguishing various conceptions of democracy. I distinguish a majoritarian (多数主义的) or statistical conception from what I call the *partnership* conception. The latter holds that in a genuinely democratic community each citizen participates as an equal partner, which means more than just that he has an equal vote. It means that he has an equal voice and an equal stake in the result. On that conception, which I defend, democracy itself requires the protection of just those individual rights to justice and liberty that democracy is sometimes said to threaten.

(1151 words)

New Words

reigning	[ˈreɪnɪŋ]	*adj.*	exercising power or authority 起支配作用的
dominion	[dəˈmɪnjən]	*n.*	dominance or power through legal authority 支配
laissez-faire	[ˌleseɪˈfeə]	*adj.*	with minimally restricted freedom in commerce 自由放任的
impoverish	[ɪmˈpɒvərɪʃ]	*v.*	make poor 使贫穷
regulatory	[ˈregjʊlətərɪ]	*adj.*	restricting according to rules or principles 管理的,调整的
endowment	[ɪnˈdaʊmənt]	*n.*	natural abilities or qualities 天赋,才能
posture	[ˈpɒstʃə]	*n.*	a rationalized mental attitude 态度,情形
auction	[ˈɔːkʃən]	*n.*	the public sale of something to the highest bidder 拍卖
endorse	[ɪnˈdɔːs]	*v.*	give support or one's approval to 支持,赞同
taxation	[tækˈseɪʃən]	*n.*	the imposition of taxes; the practice of the government in levying taxes on the subjects of a state 课税,征税
partnership	[ˈpɑːtnəʃɪp]	*n.*	a cooperative relationship between people or groups who agree to share responsibility for achieving some specific goal 合作关系

New Expressions

subscribe to	agree to 同意
in terms of	according to, in the light of 依据，按照
be entitled to	be qualified for 有资格
with an eye to	considering 着眼于
at leisure	unhurriedly 从容地，闲着地
in consequence	therefore 因此，结果
call for	require 要求，需要
on this account	for this reason 因此，由于这个原因
on grounds (of)	on the basis of 以……为理由，根据
on this view	from the point of view of 从这一观点来看

Ronald Dworkin, (December 11, 1931—February 14, 2013) was an American philosopher and scholar of constitutional law. He was Frank Henry Sommer Professor of Law and Philosophy at New York University and Professor of Jurisprudence at University College London, and had taught previously at Yale Law School and the University of Oxford. According to a survey in *The Journal of Legal Studies*, Dworkin was the second most-cited American legal scholar of the twentieth century. His theory of law as integrity, in which judges interpret the law in terms of consistent and communal moral principles, especially justice and fairness, is among the most influential contemporary theories about the nature of law. Dworkin advocated a "moral reading" of the United States Constitution, and an interpretivist approach to law and morality.

Task 1 Questions for Comprehension

Directions: Please answer the following questions based on Text B.

1. What are the two reigning principles that render a government legitimate?
2. Why is there no politically neutral distribution?
3. Why did the author think a laissez-faire political economy violates the second principle?
4. What's the problem with the practice of making wealth equal no matter what choices people made for themselves?
5. What did the author want to show by imagining the initial auction of all available resources?
6. What kind of theory of liberty did the author argue for?
7. How could the author's theory of liberty eliminate the conflict between equality and liberty?
8. How can you tell positive liberty from negative liberty?
9. How does a partnership conception of democracy differ from a majoritarian or statistical conception of democracy?

10. Why did the author say that a partnership conception of democracy avoids the conflict between equality and democracy?

Task 2　Questions for Discussion
Directions: Discuss the following questions in pairs or groups.
1. How do you understand equality, liberty and democracy? How are they related?
2. Discuss these questions with your partner(s) in class.

Part Four　Cross Cultural Communication

Passage A

"仁"和"礼"

　　孔子常言仁,仁即是人心。孔子言仁,又常兼言智,智即是人心之明。孔子言仁,又常兼言礼,礼则是人之生命之体。《诗》曰:"相鼠有体,人而无礼。"鼠之生命,必有一体。岂人之生命乃可无体? 一般以人身为人生之体,但此身之生至短暂,至渺小,亦何以胜于鼠之体。中国人则以礼为人生之体,人生必寄于礼以为体。礼乃人类大生命之体,身则仅为人类小生命之体。鼠则仅知有小生命,人则应知更有大生命。

　　何谓礼? 人与人相交始有礼。人之初生即有交,惟父母兄妹。有子曰:"孝弟也者,其为仁之本欤。"实则此仁即是人之本,亦即是礼之本。人生最先一大别曰长幼。中国人有成人之礼,男二十,女十八,始称为成人。方其幼,则未得为成人;然其时则已有礼。礼尚往来,但未成人,则其与人交,乃有来而无往。惟此心之孝弟,对其父母兄妹,则惟有服从,更无反抗。今人不好言服从,但非服从,则幼小又何得成人。及其年长成人,仍得服从。饥欲食,渴欲饮,此乃天命,亦自知服从。故服从亦即人之天性。中国人常言孝顺,顺亦即是服从。中国人之礼,亦多主服从,不主反抗,礼中之反抗成分则甚少。

　　人生自长幼之异外,复有男女之异。男女之结合以成夫妇,成为一体,乃为人生一大礼。倘以未成年人言,则其生命实以父母之生命为阳面,己之生命则仅为阴面。一阴一阳之为道,道即人生。非有父母,即不得成其一己之人生。倘以已成年人之言,则夫为其生命之阳,而妇为其生命之阴,夫妻结合,乃始成其两人生命之一体,即是同一生命。独阳独阴,则不成气,不为道,亦不得谓是一正常之人生。故中国人以夫妇为人伦之始。伦者,如丝之有经纶。非有经纶,丝不成物。非有男女结合,则不得谓乃人生之正常体,实则人而非人矣。

　　人之有男女,乃一自然。男女之结合为夫妇,此乃人文。人文者,犹言人生之花样。鸟兽虫鱼皆有生,但其花样少,故不得称鸟文兽文虫文鱼文。无生物更少花样,故无物文。惟天地大自然乃可称天文地文。人生花样虽多,终不能脱离自然。亦惟有服从自然,不得向之作反抗。斯则自然为阳刚面,而人文只为阴柔面。但人文日进,花样日多,则自然之对人文,有些处亦得服从,此则人文转为阳刚面,而自然则转为阴柔面。"先天而天弗违,后天而奉天时"。此又一阴一阳之为道,岂得谓在大道之中乃无服从之一义。

礼既出于仁，本于人心之自然，乃于礼中必有乐。中国人生乃一礼乐之人生，人生有一至哀不乐者，乃为人之死。生必有死，亦一自然，不可反抗。乃于人文中发明了死生相交之礼，视死如生，慎终追远，有哭有踊，有葬有祭，有坟墓有祠堂。若谓死者已上天堂，而中国人之礼乃若死者时时尚在人间。是则人文为主，而自然转为辅矣。西方宗教信仰，乃谓人死则灵魂重归天堂，此为自然乎？抑为人文乎？人生必有死，此为自然。死后灵魂归天堂，则实是反抗了自然，而亦已脱离了人文。耶稣言凯撒事凯撒管，则其教虽求脱离自然，但尚未违反及人文，惟置人文于不闻不问而已。中国死生之礼，则并未脱离自然，而显为一人文，而人心乃于此得安得乐。如孔子死，其门人弟子岂不大悲，然心丧三年，相与庐墓而居，斯则心安亦可谓一乐矣。尽其心，斯知性，斯知天，此亦依然是一自然，而人心仍亦与此得安乐，此则不得不谓乃中国人之大智矣。

（1297字）

注 解

本文选自钱穆《中国文化特质》(台北阳明山庄1983年9月版)。

Task 1　Questions for Comprehension and Discussion

Directions: Please answer the following questions.

1. How did Qian Mu elaborate on "仁" and "礼"?
2. How do you understand Qian Mu's account of "人文" and "自然"?

Task 2　Summary

Directions: One of your American friends cannot read Chinese, but he is interested in Qian Mu's philosophy. Summarize this passage.

Passage B

On Liberty[1]
John Stuart Mill[2]

The object of this essay is to assert one very simple principle, as entitled to govern absolutely the dealings of society with the individual in the way of compulsion and control, whether the means used be physical force in the form of legal penalties, or the moral coercion of public opinion. That principle is, that the sole end for which mankind are warranted, individually or collectively in interfering with the liberty of action of any of their number, is self-protection. That the only purpose for which power can be rightfully exercised over any member of a civilized community, against his will, is to prevent harm to others. His own good, either physical or moral, is not a sufficient warrant. He cannot rightfully be compelled to do or forbear because it will be better for him to do so, because it will make him happier, because, in the opinions of others, to do so would be wise, or even right. These are good reasons for remonstrating with him, or reasoning with him, or persuading him, or entreating him, but not for compelling him, or visiting him with any evil, in case he do otherwise. To justify that, the conduct from which it is desired to deter him must be calculated to produce evil to someone else. The only part of the conduct of anyone, for which he is amenable to society, is that which concerns others. In the part which merely concerns himself, his independence is, of right, absolute. Over himself, over his own body and mind, the individual is sovereign.

It is, perhaps, hardly necessary to say that this doctrine is meant to apply only to human beings in the maturity of their faculties. We are not speaking of children, or of young persons below the age which the law may fix as that of manhood or womanhood. Those who are still in a state to require being taken care of by others, must be protected against their own actions as well as against external injury. For the same reason, we may leave out of consideration those backward states of society in which the race itself may be considered as in its nonage. The early difficulties in the way of spontaneous progress are so great, that there is seldom any choice of means for overcoming them; and a ruler full of the spirit of improvement is warranted in the use of any expedients that will attain an end, perhaps otherwise unattainable. Despotism is a legitimate mode of government in dealing with barbarians, provided the end be their improvement, and the means justified by actually effecting that end. Liberty, as a principle, has no application to any state of things anterior to the time when mankind have become capable of being improved by free and equal discussion. Until then, there is nothing for them but implicit obedience to an Akbar or a Charlemagne, if they are so fortunate as to find one. But as soon as mankind have attained the capacity of being guided to their own improvement by conviction or persuasion (a period long since reached in all nations with whom we need here concern ourselves), compulsion, either in the direct form or in that of pains and penalties for non-compliance, is no longer admissible as a means to their own good, and justifiable only for the security of others.

It is proper to state that I forego any advantage which could be derived to my argument from the idea of abstract right as a thing independent of utility. I regard utility as the ultimate appeal on all ethical questions; but it must be utility in the largest sense, grounded on the permanent interests of man as a progressive being. Those interests, I contend, authorize the subjection of individual spontaneity to external control, only in respect to those actions of each, which concern the interest of other people. If any one does an act hurtful to others, there is a prima facie case for punishing him, by law, or, where legal penalties are not safely applicable, by general disapprobation. There are also many positive acts for the benefit of others, which he may rightfully be compelled to perform; such as, to give evidence in a court of justice; to bear his fair share in the common defence, or in any other joint work necessary to the interest of the society of which he enjoys the protection; and to perform certain acts of individual beneficence, such as saving a fellow-creature's life, or interposing to protect the defenceless against ill-usage, things which whenever it is obviously a man's duty to do, he may rightfully be made responsible to society for not doing. A person may cause evil to others not only by his actions but by his inaction, and in either case he is justly accountable to them for the injury. The latter case, it is true, requires a much more cautious exercise of compulsion than the former. To make any one answerable for doing evil to others, is the rule; to make him answerable for not preventing evil, is, comparatively speaking, the exception. Yet there are many cases clear enough and grave enough to justify that exception. In all things which regard the external relations of the individual, he is de jure amenable to those whose interests are concerned, and if need be, to society as their protector. There are often good reasons for not holding him to the responsibility; but these reasons must arise from the special expediencies of the case: either because it is a kind of case in which he is on the whole likely to act better, when left to his own discretion, than when controlled in any way in which society have it in their power to control him; or because the attempt to exercise control would produce other evils, greater than those which it would prevent. When such reasons as these preclude the enforcement of responsibility, the conscience of the agent himself should step into the vacant judgment-seat, and protect those interests of others which have no external protection; judging himself all the more rigidly, because the case does not admit of his being made accountable to the judgment of his fellow creatures.

But there is a sphere of action in which society, as distinguished from the individual, has, if any, only an indirect interest; comprehending all that portion of a person's life and conduct which affects only himself, or, if it also affects others, only with their free, voluntary, and undeceived consent and participation. When I say only himself, I mean directly, and in the first instance: for whatever affects himself, may affect others through himself; and the objection which may be grounded on this contingency, will receive consideration in the sequel. This, then, is the appropriate region of human liberty. It comprises, first, the inward domain of consciousness; demanding liberty of conscience, in the most comprehensive sense; liberty of thought and feeling; absolute freedom of opinion and sentiment on all subjects, practical or speculative, scientific, moral, or theological. The liberty of expressing and publishing opinions may seem to fall under a different principle, since it belongs to that part of the conduct of an individual which concerns other people; but, being almost of as much importance as the liberty of thought itself, and resting in great part on the same reasons, is practically inseparable from it. Secondly, the principle requires liberty of tastes and pursuits; of framing the plan of our life to suit our own character; of doing as we like, subject to such consequences as may follow; without impediment from our fellow-creatures, so long as what we do does not harm them even though they should think our conduct foolish, perverse, or wrong. Thirdly, from this liberty of each individual, follows the liberty, within the same limits, of combination among individuals; freedom to unite, for any purpose not involving harm to others: the persons combining being supposed to be of full age, and not forced or deceived.

No society in which these liberties are not, on the whole, respected, is free, whatever may be its form of government; and none is completely free in which they do not exist absolute and unqualified. The only freedom which deserves the name, is that of pursuing our own good in our own way, so long as we do not attempt to deprive others of theirs, or impede their efforts to obtain it. Each is the proper guardian of his own health, whether bodily, or mental or spiritual. Mankind are greater gainers by suffering each other to live as seems good to themselves, than by compelling each to live as seems good to the rest.

(1450 words)

Unit 5

 **Notes**

1. The text is excerpted from John Stuart Mill's *On Liberty* (1859). ***On Liberty*** is a philosophical work by English philosopher John Stuart Mill, originally intended as a short essay. The work applies Mill's ethical system of utilitarianism to society and the state. Mill attempts to establish standards for the relationship between authority and liberty. He emphasizes the importance of individuality which he conceived as a prerequisite to the higher pleasures—the summum bonum of Utilitarianism. Furthermore, Mill criticized the errors of past attempts to defend individuality where, for example, democratic ideals resulted in the "tyranny of the majority". Among the standards established in this work are Mill's three basic liberties of individuals, his three legitimate objections to government intervention, and his two maxims regarding the relationship of the individual to society "which together form the entire doctrine of [Mill's] Essay."

2. John Stuart Mill (20 May 1806—8 May 1873) was a British philosopher, political economist and civil servant. He was an influential contributor to social theory, political theory and political economy. He has been called "the most influential English-speaking philosopher of the nineteenth century". Mill's conception of liberty justified the freedom of the individual in opposition to unlimited state control.

Task 1   Questions for Comprehension and Discussion

Directions: Please answer the following questions.

1. What is the ethic principle that is asserted in this essay?
2. Who is this principle meant to apply to?
3. When can individual spontaneity be subjected to external control?
4. What does the appropriate region of human liberty comprise?
5. What kind of freedom can be called true freedom?

Task 2   Essay Writing

Directions: Suppose you take a class of political philosophy. Your professor asks you to write an essay in Chinese discussing the following questions:

How do you understand Mill's account of liberty? How did he develop such an account? Do you think his argument is convincing enough? Could you give more evidence to support his position? Or maybe you can advance a counter-argument to object to his position.

_____
_____
_____

Unit 6

ECONOMY AND SOCIETY

The study of his own advantage naturally, or rather necessarily, leads him to prefer that employment which is most advantageous to the society.

—*Adam Smith*

Learning Objectives

Upon the completion of this unit, you should be able to:

Remembering & Understanding	★ study the life of famous economists; ★ develop insights into the major schools of thought in economics in the social and historical context;
Analyzing & Applying	★ write a deductive essay; ★ oppose a motion by refuting arguments and constructing one's own case;
Evaluating & Creating	★ explain how ancient Chinese military wisdom is relevant for business today; ★ prepare a speech draft on the image of merchants in literature; ★ develop your understanding of the advantages and disadvantages of market economy.

Unit 6

Part One Lead-in

Section 1 Listening

Directions: Please fill in the blanks with words or sentences on the basis of what you have heard in the audio clip. Then discuss the following questions in pairs or groups.

Why Should We Study Past Economic Thinkers

Why study great economists of the past? 1_____, we've had decades or even centuries to refine their ideas and 2_____ new ideas, thinking out whether they were right or they were wrong. So 3_____ going back to the old errors, the old mistakes and the old ways of looking at things? When we go back, a lot of times we can see that the vocabulary that they are using is quaint and the arguments they are having are somewhat 4_____ or even irrelevant today. And there is no doubt that 5_____ that is true.

6. According to the lecturer, why do some people think it is useless to study past economists? What are the reasons he mentions to oppose this point of view?
7. According to the quote from Keynes, even when economists are wrong, their ideas are very powerful. What do you think of this? Work in pairs and exchange your views.
8. The recording is the opening remarks of a lecture series on great economists. Name three economists you have heard of and summarize what you know about them.

Section 2 Watching

Directions: Please watch the video clip and work on the following questions in pairs or groups.

A Beautiful Mind: The Nash Equilibrium

1. This part of the film consists of two scenes—one at the bar, and the other in the office. Retell what happens in each of the scenes. Add some details using your imagination if necessary.
2. Take the example from the film to explain why, according to Nash, "Adam Smith was wrong".
3. What do you know about John Nash? What are his major contributions to economics?

Part Two Reading and Writing

Pre-Reading Questions

1. What are the costs and benefits of free trade? What are the barriers to free trade?
2. What does "an invisible hand" usually refer to? In what ways is it "invisible"? What kind of role does it play in trade?

Text A

Individuals in Foreign Trade[1]
Adam Smith[2]

1   Every individual is continually *exerting himself* to find out the most advantageous employment for whatever *capital* he can command. It is his own advantage, indeed, and not that of the society, which he has in view. But the study of his own advantage naturally, or rather necessarily, leads him to prefer that employment which is most advantageous to the society.

2   First, every individual *endeavours* to employ his capital as near home as he can, and *consequently* as much as he can in the support of domestic industry; provided always that he can thereby obtain the ordinary, or not a great deal less than the ordinary profits of *stock*.

3   Thus, upon equal or nearly equal profits, every *wholesale* merchant naturally prefers the home-trade to the foreign trade of consumption, and the foreign trade of consumption to the *carrying trade*. In the home-trade his capital is never so long out of his sight as it frequently is in the foreign trade of consumption. He can know better the character and situation of the persons whom he trusts, and if he should happen to be *deceived*, he knows better the laws of the country from which he must seek *redress*. In the carrying trade, the capital of the merchant is, as it were, divided between two foreign countries, and no part of it is ever necessarily brought home, or placed under his own immediate view and command. The capital which an Amsterdam merchant *employs* in carrying corn from Konigsberg(哥尼斯堡,俄罗斯西部港市加里宁格勒的旧称) to Lisbon, and fruit and wine from Lisbon to Konigsberg, must generally be the one half of it at Konigsberg and the other half at Lisbon. No part of it need ever come to Amsterdam. The natural residence of such a merchant should either be at Konigsberg or Lisbon, and it can only be some very particular circumstances which can make him prefer the residence of Amsterdam. The uneasiness, however, which he feels at being separated so far from his capital generally determines him to bring part both of the Konigsberg goods which he *destines* for the market of Lisbon, and of the Lisbon goods which he destines for that of Konigsberg, to Amsterdam: and though this necessarily *subjects him to* a double *charge* of *loading* and unloading, as well as to the payment of some duties and *customs*, yet *for the sake of* having some part of his capital always under his own view and command, he willingly *submits* to this extraordinary charge; and it is in this manner that every country which has any considerable share of the carrying trade becomes always the *emporium*, or general market, for the goods of all the different countries whose trade it carries on. The merchant, in order to save a second loading and unloading, endeavours always to sell in the home-market as much of the goods of all those different countries as he can, and thus, so far as he can, to *convert* his carrying trade

into a foreign trade of consumption. A merchant, in the same manner, who is engaged in the foreign trade of consumption, when he collects goods for foreign markets, will always be glad, upon equal or nearly equal profits, to sell as great a part of them at home as he can. He saves himself the risk and trouble of exportation, when, so far as he can, he thus converts his foreign trade of consumption into a home-trade. Home is in this manner the centre, if I may say so, round which the capitals of the inhabitants of every country are continually circulating, and towards which they are always tending, though by particular causes they may sometimes be *driven off* and *repelled* from it towards more distant employments. But a capital employed in the home-trade, it already has been shown, necessarily *puts into motion* a greater quantity of domestic industry, and gives *revenue* and employment to a greater number of the inhabitants of the country, than an equal capital employed in the foreign trade of consumption: and one employed in the foreign trade of consumption has the same advantage over an equal capital employed in the carrying trade. Upon equal, or only nearly equal profits, therefore, every individual naturally *inclines* to employ his capital in the manner in which it is likely to afford the greatest support to domestic industry, and to give revenue and employment to the greatest number of people of his own country.

Secondly, every individual who employs his capital in the support of domestic industry, necessarily endeavours so to direct that industry that its produce may be of the greatest possible value.

The produce of industry is what it adds to the subject or materials upon which it is employed. *In proportion* as the value of this produce is great or small, so will likewise be the profits of the employer. But it is only for the sake of profit that any man employs a capital in the support of industry; and he will always, therefore, endeavour to employ it in the support of that industry of which the produce is likely to be of the greatest value, or to exchange for the greatest quantity either of money or of other goods.

But the annual revenue of every society is always precisely equal to the exchangeable value of the whole annual produce of its industry, or rather is precisely the same thing with that exchangeable value. As every individual, therefore, endeavours as much as he can both to employ his capital in the support of domestic industry, and so to direct that industry that its produce may be of the greatest value; every individual necessarily labours to render the annual revenue of the society as great as he can. He generally, indeed, neither intends to promote the public interest, nor knows how much he is promoting it. By preferring the support of domestic to that of foreign industry, he intends only his own security; and by directing that industry in such a manner as its produce may be of the greatest value, he intends only his own gain, and he is in this, as in many other cases, led by an invisible hand to promote an end which was no part of his intention. Nor is it always the worse for the society that it was no part of it. By pursuing his own interest he frequently promotes that of the society more *effectually* than when he really intends to promote it. I have never known much good done by those who *affected* to trade for the public good. It is an *affectation*, indeed, not very common among merchants, and very few words need be employed in *dissuading* them from it.

(1115 words)

New Words

capital	['kæpɪtəl]	n.	buildings or machinery which are necessary to produce goods or to make companies more efficient, but which do not make money directly 资产
endeavour	[ɪn'dɛvə]	v.	try very hard to do something 努力
consequently	['kɒnsɪkwəntlɪ]	adv.	as a result 结果
stock	[stɒk]	n.	the total amount of goods which it has available to sell 存货
wholesale	['həʊl‚seɪl]	n.	the activity of buying and selling goods in large quantities and therefore at cheaper prices, usually to stores who then sell them to the public 批发
deceive	[dɪ'siːv]	v.	make someone believe something that is not true, usually in order to get some advantage for yourself 欺骗
redress	[rɪ'drɛs]	n.	money that someone pays you because they have caused you harm or loss 赔款, 赔偿
employ	[ɪm'plɔɪ]	v.	use 使用
destine	['dɛstɪn]	v.	to set apart or appoint (for a certain purpose or person, or to do something) 指定
charge	[tʃɑːdʒ]	n.	an amount of money that you have to pay for a service 费用
load	[ləʊd]	v.	put a large quantity of things into a vehicle or a container (向车辆或容器里) 大量装入, 装载
customs	['kʌstəmz]	n.	taxes that people pay for importing and exporting goods 关税
submit	[səb'mɪt]	v.	allow something to be done to you, or you do what somebody wants, for example because you are not powerful enough to resist 屈从
emporium	[ɛm'pɔːrɪəm]	n.	general market, fair 商场
convert	[kən'vɜːt]	v.	change into a different form 转变
repel	[rɪ'pɛl]	v.	drive back 驱逐, 推开
revenue	['rɛvɪ‚njuː]	n.	income 收入
incline	[ɪn'klaɪn]	v.	tend 倾向于
effectually	[ɪ'fɛktjʊəlɪ]	adv.	with a striking effect; thoroughly 有效地, 全面地

Unit 6

affect	[əˈfɛkt]	v.	put on an appearance or show of; make a pretence of 假装
affectation	[ˌæfɛkˈteɪʃən]	n.	something that is not genuine or natural, but is intended to impress other people 娇柔做作
dissuade	[dɪˈsweɪd]	v.	persuade somebody not to do or believe something 劝阻

New Expressions

exert oneself	make a great physical or mental effort, or work hard to do something 耗费（自己的精力）
carrying trade	the business of transporting commercial goods from one place to another by land, sea, or air 海外贸易，转口贸易
subject sb. to	to make someone experience something unpleasant 使某人经受
for the sake of	for the purpose of 为了
drive off	force to go away 赶走
put into motion	to make a series of events or a process start happening 启动
in proportion	showing the correct size or proportion relative to something else 成比例

1. This text is an excerpt from *An Inquiry into the Nature and Causes of the Wealth of Nations* (1776), generally referred to by its shortened title *The Wealth of Nations* and considered the first modern work of economics. The book offers one of the world's first collected descriptions of what builds nations' wealth and is today a fundamental work in classical economics. By reflecting upon the economics at the beginning of the Industrial Revolution, the book touches upon such broad topics as the division of labor, productivity, and free markets.

2. Adam Smith (5 June 1723—17 July 1790), the author of the text, was a Scottish moral philosopher, pioneer of political economy, and key Scottish Enlightenment figure. Often cited as the "father of modern economics", Adam Smith is still among the most influential thinkers in the field of economics today.

Task 1 Generating the Outline

Directions: Please identify the thesis of the passage and the main point of each paragraph, and then find out how these points develop the thesis.

_____
_____
_____
_____

Task 2　Understanding the Text

Directions: Please answer the following questions based on Text A.

1. Upon equal or nearly equal profits, why do wholesale merchants naturally prefer the home-trade to the foreign trade, and the foreign trade to the carrying trade?
2. Why does the merchant doing the carrying trade between Konigsberg and Lisbon bring some of the goods to Amsterdam—his hometown?
3. If someone focuses on the foreign trade, does he do less good to the home society than those who do domestic trade?
4. Why do merchants trade? What is the author's attitude towards those who affected to trade for the public good?

Task 3　Learning the Phrases

Directions: Please fill in the blanks in the sentences below with the phrases listed in the box. Change the forms if necessary.

for the sake of　　subject sb to　　in propotion　　drive off　　put into motion

1. In the crisis, the workers lost their job when their former boss _____ the land.
2. Most people feel that a mayor's prominence ought to _____ a higher standard.
3. With a push of the red button, a chain of events will be _____.
4. _____ keeping things simple, we'll stick to the models that seem truly promising.
5. Some people are happy _____ as they are noticed.

Task 4　Translating the Sentences

Directions: Please translate the following sentences into Chinese.

1. Every individual is continually exerting himself to find out the most advantageous employment for whatever capital he can command.

2. Home is in this manner the centre, if I may say so, round which the capitals of the inhabitants of every country are continually circulating, and towards which they are always tending...

Unit 6

3. The produce of industry is what it adds to the subject or materials upon which it is employed.

4. By directing that industry in such a manner as its produce may be of the greatest value, he intends only his own gain, and he is in this, as in many other cases, led by an invisible hand to promote an end which was no part of his intention.

5. It is an affectation, indeed, not very common among merchants, and very few words need be employed in dissuading them from it.

Task 5 Writing Exercises

Directions: Discuss the following question with a partner.

If merchants are profit-driven and it is good for the society, why do many companies donate for schools, sponsor environmental campaigns and spend on other aspects of public welfare?

Directions: Write an essay in 300 words to express your point of view on the above topic.

Part Three Reading and Speaking

Pre-Reading Questions

1. What happened during the Great Depression in the 1930s?
2. How did the financial crisis in 2008 begin? What were the consequences of the crisis?

How Did Economists Get It So Wrong?[1]
Paul Krugman[2]

I. MISTAKING BEAUTY FOR TRUTH

1 It's hard to believe now, but not long ago economists were congratulating themselves over the success of their field. Those successes—or so they believed—were both theoretical and practical, leading to a golden era for the profession.

2 Last year, everything came apart.

3 Few economists saw our current crisis coming, but this *predictive* failure was the least of the field's problems. More important was the profession's blindness to the very possibility of *catastrophic* failures in a market economy. During the golden years, financial economists came to believe that markets were *inherently* stable—indeed, that stocks and other *assets* were always priced just right. There was nothing in the *prevailing* models suggesting the possibility of the kind of collapse that happened last year. Meanwhile, macroeconomists were divided in their views. But the main division was between those who insisted that free-market economies never go *astray* and those who believed that economies may *stray* now and then but that any major *deviations* from the path of prosperity could and would be corrected by the all-powerful Fed(美联储). Neither side was prepared to cope with an economy that went off the rails despite the Fed's best efforts.

4 What happened to the economics profession? And where does it go from here?

5 As I see it, the economics profession went astray because economists, as a group, mistook beauty, *clad* in impressive-looking mathematics, for truth. Until the Great Depression, most economists clung to a vision of capitalism as a perfect or nearly perfect system. That vision wasn't sustainable in the face of mass unemployment, but as memories of the Depression faded, economists fell back in love with the old, idealized vision of an economy in which rational individuals interact in perfect markets, this time *gussied up* with fancy equations. The renewed romance with the idealized market was, to be sure, partly a response to shifting political winds, partly a response to financial *incentives*. But while *sabbaticals* at the Hoover Institution and job opportunities on Wall Street are *nothing to sneeze at*, the central cause of the profession's failure was the desire for an *all-encompassing*, intellectually elegant approach that also gave economists a chance to show off their mathematical *prowess*.

6 Unfortunately, this romanticized and *sanitized* vision of the economy led most economists to ignore all the things that can go wrong. They turned a blind eye to the limitations of human rationality that often lead to bubbles and *busts*; to the problems of institutions that *run amok*; to the imperfections of markets—especially financial markets—that can cause the economy's operating system to undergo sudden, unpredictable crashes; and to the dangers created when regulators don't believe in

regulation.

7   It's much harder to say where the economics profession goes from here. But what's almost certain is that economists will have to learn to live with *messiness*. That is, they will have to acknowledge the importance of irrational and often unpredictable behavior, face up to the often *idiosyncratic* imperfections of markets and accept that an elegant economic "theory of everything" is a long way off. In practical terms, this will translate into more cautious policy advice—and a reduced willingness to *dismantle* economic safeguards in the faith that markets will solve all problems.

II. FROM SMITH TO KEYNES AND BACK

8   The birth of economics as a discipline is usually credited to Adam Smith, who published "The Wealth of Nations" in 1776. Over the next 160 years an extensive body of economic theory was developed, whose central message was: Trust the market. Yes, economists admitted that there were cases in which markets might fail, of which the most important was the case of "externalities"—costs that people impose on others without paying the price, like traffic *congestion* or pollution. But the basic presumption of "neoclassical" economics (named after the late-19th-century theorists who elaborated on the concepts of their "classical" *predecessors*) was that we should have faith in the market system.

9   This faith was, however, *shattered* by the Great Depression. Actually, even in the face of total collapse some economists insisted that whatever happens in a market economy must be right: "Depressions are not simply evils," declared Joseph Schumpeter in 1934—1934! They are, he added, "forms of something which has to be done." But many, and eventually most, economists turned to the insights of John Maynard Keynes for both an explanation of what had happened and a solution to future depressions.

    Keynes did not, despite what you may have heard, want the government to run the economy. He described his analysis in his 1936 masterwork, "The General Theory of Employment, Interest and Money," as "moderately conservative in its implications." He wanted to fix capitalism, not replace it. But he did challenge the notion that free-market economies can function without a minder, expressing particular *contempt* for financial markets, which he viewed as being dominated by short-term *speculation* with little regard for fundamentals. And he called for active government intervention—printing more money and, if necessary, spending heavily on public works—to fight unemployment during *slumps*.

    It's important to understand that Keynes did much more than make bold assertions. "The General Theory" is a work of profound, deep analysis—analysis that persuaded the best young economists of the day. Yet the story of economics over the past half century is, to a large degree, the story of a retreat from Keynesianism and a return to neoclassicism. The neoclassical revival was initially led by Milton Friedman of the University of Chicago, who asserted as early as 1953 that neoclassical economics works well enough as a description of the way the economy actually functions to be "both extremely fruitful and deserving of much confidence." But what about depressions?

12   Friedman's counterattack against Keynes began with the doctrine known as *monetarism*. Monetarists didn't disagree in principle with the idea that a market economy needs deliberate stabilization. "We are all Keynesians now," Friedman once said, although he later claimed he was quoted out of context. Monetarists asserted, however, that a very limited, circumscribed（受限制的）form of government intervention—namely, instructing central banks to keep the nation's money supply, the sum of cash in circulation and bank deposits, growing on a steady path—is all that's required to prevent depressions. Famously, Friedman and his *collaborator*, Anna Schwartz, argued that if the Federal Reserve had done its job properly, the Great Depression would not have happened. Later, Friedman made a compelling case against any deliberate effort by government to push unemployment below its "natural" level (currently thought to be about 4.8 percent in the United States): excessively expansionary policies, he predicted, would lead to a combination of inflation and high unemployment—a prediction that was *borne out* by the *stagflation* of the 1970s, which greatly advanced the credibility of the anti-Keynesian movement.

13   Eventually, however, the anti-Keynesian counterrevolution went far beyond Friedman's position, which came to seem relatively moderate compared with what his successors were saying. Among financial economists, Keynes's *disparaging* vision of financial markets as a *"casino"* was replaced by "efficient market" theory, which asserted that financial markets always get asset prices right given the available information. Meanwhile, many macroeconomists completely rejected Keynes's framework for understanding economic slumps. Some returned to the view of Schumpeter and other apologists for the Great Depression, viewing recessions as a good thing, part of the economy's adjustment to change. And even those not willing to go that far argued that any attempt to fight an economic slump would do more harm than good.

14   Not all macroeconomists were willing to go down this road: many became self-described New Keynesians, who continued to believe in an active role for the government. Yet even they mostly accepted the notion that investors and consumers are rational and that markets generally get it right.

15   Of course, there were exceptions to these trends: a few economists challenged the assumption of rational behavior, questioned the belief that financial markets can be trusted and pointed to the long history of financial crises that had *devastating* economic consequences. But they were swimming against the tide, unable to *make* much *headway* against a *pervasive* and, *in retrospect*, foolish *complacency*.

(*1348 words*)

Unit 6

New Words

predictive	[prɪˈdɪktɪv]	*adj.*	concerned with determining what will happen in the future 预言性的, 预测性的
catastrophic	[ˌkætəˈstrɒfɪk]	*adj.*	involving or causing a sudden terrible disaster 灾难性的
inherently	[ɪnˈhɪərəntlɪ]	*adj.*	necessarily and naturally 内在地
asset	[ˈæset]	*n.*	all the things that a company or a person owns 资产
prevailing	[prɪˈveɪlɪŋ]	*adj.*	generally current; widespread 主要的
astray	[əˈstreɪ]	*adv.*	away from the right or good 误入歧途地
stray	[streɪ]	*v.*	go in the wrong direction 迷失
deviation	[ˌdiːvɪˈeɪʃən]	*n.*	doing something that is different from what people consider to be normal or acceptable 偏离; 越轨
clad	[klæd]	*adj.*	being covered 被……所遮盖
incentive	[ɪnˈsentɪv]	*n.*	something that encourages you to do something 鼓励措施
sabbatical	[səˈbætɪkəl]	*n.*	a period of time during which somebody such as a university teacher can leave their ordinary work and travel or study (大学教师等的) 休假
all-encompassing	[ˈɔːlenˈkʌmpəsɪŋ]	*adj.*	broad in scope or content 包罗万象的
prowess	[ˈpraʊɪs]	*n.*	great skill at doing something 杰出的技能
sanitized	[ˈsænɪtaɪzd]	*adj.*	clean 洁净的, 纯净的
bust	[bʌst]	*n.*	break 破裂
messiness	[ˈmesɪnɪs]	*n.*	untidiness 混乱, 肮脏
idiosyncratic	[ˌɪdɪəʊsɪŋˈkrætɪk]	*adj.*	unusual 怪异的; 另类的
dismantle	[dɪsˈmæntəl]	*v.*	cause something to stop functioning by gradually reducing its power or purpose 逐步废除
congestion	[kənˈdʒestʃən]	*n.*	traffic jam 拥塞, 堵塞
predecessor	[ˈpredəsesə]	*n.*	forerunner, ancestor 前任, 前辈
shatter	[ˈʃætə]	*v.*	completely destroy (dreams, hopes, or beliefs) 粉碎 (梦想、希望、信仰等)
contempt	[kənˈtempt]	*n.*	lack of respect (for someone or something) 轻蔑, 鄙视
speculation	[spekjəˈleɪʃən]	*n.*	investment involving high risk but also possibility of high profits 投机
slump	[slʌmp]	*n.*	a time when many people in a country are unemployed and poor 经济萧条时期
monetarism	[ˈmʌnɪtəˌrɪzəm]	*n.*	an economic policy that involves controlling the amount of money that is available and in use in a country at any one time 货币控制政策
collaborator	[kəˈlæbəreɪtə]	*n.*	someone that you work with to produce a piece of work, especially a book or some research 合作者, 合著者

stagflation	[stægˈfleɪʃən]	n.	If an economy is suffering from stagflation, inflation is high but there is no increase in the demand for goods or in the number of people who have jobs 滞胀
disparaging	[dɪˈspærɪdʒɪŋ]	adj.	criticizing someone, in a way that shows you do not respect or value them 贬损的
casino	[kəˈsiːnəʊ]	n.	a building or room where people play gambling games such as roulette 赌场
devastating	[ˈdevəsteɪtɪŋ]	adj.	highly destructive, crushing 毁灭性的
pervasive	[pəˈveɪsɪv]	adj.	widespread 遍布的,弥漫的
complacency	[kəmˈpleɪsənsi]	n.	being complacent about a situation 自满

New Expressions

gussy up	dressed in a fancy or very fashionable way 精心打扮,盛装
nothing to sneeze at	something that deserves serious attention 不容小视
run amok [əˈmɒk]	run wild 发狂
bear out	support 支持,证实
make headway	progress toward achieving something 取得进展
in retrospect	When you consider something in retrospect, you think about it afterward, and often have a different opinion about it from the one that you had at the time. 回想

Notes

1. This text is an excerpt from an article in the *New York Times* in 2009 after the global financial crisis erupted in 2008.
2. Paul Krugman, the author of the text, is an American economist. In 2008, Krugman won the Nobel Memorial Prize in Economic Sciences for his analysis of trade patterns and location of economic activity.

Task 1 Questions for Comprehension

Directions: Please answer the following questions based on Text B.

1. According to the author, what are economists good at? What are the things that they ignore?
2. According to the author, where does the economics profession go from here?
3. In the second part of the text, the author traces the history of economics and examines the main schools of thought in the social and historical context. Find out the economists mentioned by the author and summarize their points of view. Arrange your answer chronologically.
4. What is the author's attitude towards those who challenged the assumption of rational behavior and distrusted the financial markets?

Task 2 Questions for Discussion

Directions: Discuss the following questions in pairs or groups.

1. Set out possible arguments for the motion "making trade fairer is more important than making it freer." Vote in class for three of the strongest arguments for a proposition case.
2. Deliver a five-minute speech to refute the chosen arguments in the exercise above and present your arguments to oppose the motion. The following outline may help you structure your speech.
    -Addressing the audience
    -Refuting the chosen arguments on the propositional side
    -Developing constructive arguments
    -Closing remarks

Part Four Cross Cultural Communication

Passage A

孙子兵法[1]

孙斌[2]

始计第一

孙子曰:兵者,国之大事,死生之地,存亡之道,不可不察也。故经之以五事,校之以计,而索其情:一曰道,二曰天,三曰地,四曰将,五曰法。道者,令民于上同意,可与之死,可与之生,而不危也;天者,阴阳、寒暑、时制也;地者,远近、险易、广狭、死生也;将者,智、信、仁、勇、严也;法者,曲制、官道、主用也。凡此五者,将莫不闻,知之者胜,不知之者不胜。故校之以计,而索其情,曰:主孰有道?将孰有能?天地孰得?法令孰行?兵众孰强?士卒孰练?赏罚孰明?吾以此知胜负矣。将听吾计,用之必胜,留之;将不听吾计,用之必败,去之。计利以听,乃为之势,以佐其外。势者,因利而制权也。兵者,诡道也。故能而示之不能,用而示之不用,近而示之远,远而示之近。利而诱之,乱而取之,实而备之,强而避之,怒而挠之,卑而骄之,佚而劳之,亲而离之,攻其无备,出其不意。此兵家之胜,不可先传也。夫未战而庙算胜者,得算多也;未战而庙算不胜者,得算少也。多算胜,少算不胜,而况于无算乎!吾以此观之,胜负见矣。

谋攻第三

孙子曰:夫用兵之法,全国为上,破国次之;全军为上,破军次之;全旅为上,破旅次之;全卒为上,破卒次之;全伍为上,破伍次之。是故百战百胜,非善之善也;不战而屈人之兵,善之善者也。故上兵伐谋,其次伐交,其次伐兵,其下攻城。攻城之法,为不得已。修橹轒辒,具器械,三月而后成;距堙,又三月而后已。将不胜其忿而蚁附之,杀士卒三分之一,而城不拔者,此攻之灾也。故善用兵者,屈人之兵而非战也,拔人之城而非攻也,毁人之国而非久也,必以全争于天下,故兵不顿而利可全,此谋攻之法也。故用兵之法,十则围之,五则攻之,倍则分之,敌则能战之,少则能逃之,不若则能避之。故小敌之坚,大敌之擒也。夫将者,国之辅也。辅周则国必强,辅隙则国必弱。故君之所以患于军者三:不知军之不可以进而谓之进,不知军之不可以退而谓之退,是谓縻军;不知三军之事而同三军之政,则军士惑矣;不知三军之权而同三军之任,则军士疑矣。三军既惑且疑,则诸侯之难至矣。是谓乱军引胜。故知胜有五:知可以战与不可以战者胜,识众寡之用者胜,上下同欲者胜,以虞待不虞者胜,将能而君不御者胜。此五者,知胜之道也。故曰:知彼知己,百战不殆;不知彼而知己,一胜一负;不知彼不知己,每战必败。

(939字)

1. 《孙子兵法》是中国现存最早的兵书,也是世界上最早的军事著作,被誉为"兵学圣典"。近年来,其中的军事思想和策略分析更吸引了包括政治学家、心理学家、信息学家和经济学家在内的广泛关注。全文共六千字左右,分为十三篇。《始计篇》为首篇,《谋攻篇》为第三篇。
2. 孙武(约公元前545年—公元前470年),字长卿,齐国乐安人,春秋时期著名的军事家、政治家,后世尊称为兵圣。

Task 1　Questions for Comprehension and Discussion

Directions: Please answer the following questions.

1. What is the attitude of Sun Tzu towards war? Why does he emphasize that "war is a very grave matter for the state and must not be commenced without due consideration."(兵者,国之大事,死生之地,存亡之道,不可不察也。)?
2. What are the five fundamental factors and seven elements that determine the outcomes of war?
3. According to Sun Tzu, what kind of commander can be called "a skillful leader (善用兵者)"?
4. Some people say business is war. In what ways is business similar to war? What can business people learn from the *Art of War*?

Task 2　Summary

Directions: Recently your friend Michael from the United States heard that the Art of War, an ancient military guide, has inspired business people today. He was very interested in the book and asked you what the book is about and why it is relevant for business today. Write a 300-word email in English to help Michael understand the tactics from the text and give one or two examples to illustrate how they can be applied as business strategies.

Unit 6

Passage B

The Merchant of Venice[1]

William Shakespeare[2]

ACT 1 SCENE III. Venice. A public place.

Enter BASSANIO and SHYLOCK

SHYLOCK

Three thousand ducats; well.

BASSANIO

Ay, sir, for three months.

SHYLOCK

For three months; well.

BASSANIO

For the which, as I told you, Antonio shall be bound.

SHYLOCK

Antonio shall become bound; well.

BASSANIO

May you stead me? will you pleasure me? shall I know your answer?

SHYLOCK

Three thousand ducats for three months and Antonio bound.

BASSANIO

Your answer to that.

SHYLOCK

Antonio is a good man.

BASSANIO

Have you heard any imputation to the contrary?

SHYLOCK

Oh, no, no, no, no: my meaning in saying he is a good man is to have you understand me that he is sufficient. Yet his means are in supposition: he hath an argosy bound to Tripolis, another to the Indies; I understand moreover, upon the Rialto, he hath a third at Mexico, a fourth for England, and other ventures he hath, squandered abroad. But ships are but boards, sailors but men: there be land-rats and water-rats, water-thieves and land-thieves, I mean pirates, and then there is the peril of waters, winds and rocks. The man is, notwithstanding, sufficient. Three thousand ducats; I think I may take his bond.

BASSANIO

Be assured you may.

SHYLOCK

I will be assured I may; and, that I may be assured, I will bethink me. May I speak with Antonio?

BASSANIO

If it please you to dine with us.

SHYLOCK

Yes, to smell pork; to eat of the habitation which your prophet the Nazarite conjured the devil into. I will buy with you, sell with you, talk with you, walk with you, and so following, but I will not eat with you, drink with you, nor pray with you. What news on the Rialto? Who is he comes here?

Enter ANTONIO

BASSANIO

This is Signior Antonio.

SHYLOCK

[Aside] How like a fawning publican he looks!
I hate him for he is a Christian,
But more for that in low simplicity
He lends out money gratis and brings down
The rate of usance here with us in Venice.
If I can catch him once upon the hip,
I will feed fat the ancient grudge I bear him.
He hates our sacred nation, and he rails,
Even there where merchants most do congregate,
On me, my bargains and my well-won thrift,
Which he calls interest. Cursed be my tribe,
If I forgive him!

BASSANIO

Shylock, do you hear?

SHYLOCK

I am debating of my present store,
And, by the near guess of my memory,
I cannot instantly raise up the gross
Of full three thousand ducats. What of that?
Tubal, a wealthy Hebrew of my tribe,
Will furnish me. But soft! how many months
Do you desire?

Unit 6

To ANTONIO
Rest you fair, good signior;
Your worship was the last man in our mouths.

ANTONIO
Shylock, although I neither lend nor borrow
By taking nor by giving of excess,
Yet, to supply the ripe wants of my friend,
I'll break a custom. Is he yet possess'd
How much ye would?
SHYLOCK
Ay, ay, three thousand ducats.
ANTONIO
And for three months.
SHYLOCK
I had forgot; three months; you told me so.
Well then, your bond; and let me see; but hear you;
Methought you said you neither lend nor borrow
Upon advantage.
ANTONIO
I do never use it.
SHYLOCK
When Jacob grazed his uncle Laban's sheep—
This Jacob from our holy Abram was,
As his wise mother wrought in his behalf,
The third possessor; ay, he was the third—
ANTONIO
And what of him? did he take interest?
SHYLOCK
No, not take interest, not, as you would say,
Directly interest: mark what Jacob did.
When Laban and himself were compromised
That all the eanlings which were streak'd and pied
Should fall as Jacob's hire, the ewes, being rank,
In the end of autumn turned to the rams,
And, when the work of generation was
Between these woolly breeders in the act,
The skilful shepherd peel'd me certain wands,
And, in the doing of the deed of kind,
He stuck them up before the fulsome ewes,
Who then conceiving did in eaning time

Fall parti-colour'd lambs, and those were Jacob's.

This was a way to thrive, and he was blest:

And thrift is blessing, if men steal it not.

ANTONIO

This was a venture, sir, that Jacob served for;

A thing not in his power to bring to pass,

But sway'd and fashion'd by the hand of heaven.

Was this inserted to make interest good?

Or is your gold and silver ewes and rams?

SHYLOCK

I cannot tell; I make it breed as fast:

But note me, signior.

ANTONIO

Mark you this, Bassanio,

The devil can cite Scripture for his purpose.

An evil soul producing holy witness

Is like a villain with a smiling cheek,

A goodly apple rotten at the heart:

O, what a goodly outside falsehood hath!

SHYLOCK

Three thousand ducats; 'tis a good round sum.

Three months from twelve; then, let me see; the rate--

ANTONIO

Well, Shylock, shall we be beholding to you?

SHYLOCK

Signior Antonio, many a time and oft

In the Rialto you have rated me

About my moneys and my usances:

Still have I borne it with a patient shrug,

For sufferance is the badge of all our tribe.

You call me misbeliever, cut-throat dog,

And spit upon my Jewish gaberdine,

And all for use of that which is mine own.

Well then, it now appears you need my help:

Go to, then; you come to me, and you say

'Shylock, we would have moneys:' you say so;

You, that did void your rheum upon my beard

And foot me as you spurn a stranger cur

Over your threshold: moneys is your suit

What should I say to you? Should I not say

'Hath a dog money? is it possible

A cur can lend three thousand ducats?' Or
Shall I bend low and in a bondman's key,
With bated breath and whispering humbleness, Say this;
'Fair sir, you spit on me on Wednesday last;
You spurn'd me such a day; another time
You call'd me dog; and for these courtesies
I'll lend you thus much moneys'?

ANTONIO

I am as like to call thee so again,
To spit on thee again, to spurn thee too.
If thou wilt lend this money, lend it not
As to thy friends; for when did friendship take
A breed for barren metal of his friend?
But lend it rather to thine enemy,
Who, if he break, thou mayst with better face
Exact the penalty.

SHYLOCK

Why, look you, how you storm!
I would be friends with you and have your love,
Forget the shames that you have stain'd me with,
Supply your present wants and take no doit
Of usance for my moneys, and you'll not hear me:
This is kind I offer.

BASSANIO

This were kindness.

SHYLOCK

This kindness will I show.
Go with me to a notary, seal me there
Your single bond; and, in a merry sport,
If you repay me not on such a day,
In such a place, such sum or sums as are
Express'd in the condition, let the forfeit
Be nominated for an equal pound
Of your fair flesh, to be cut off and taken
In what part of your body pleaseth me.

ANTONIO

Content, in faith: I'll seal to such a bond
And say there is much kindness in the Jew.

BASSANIO

You shall not seal to such a bond for me:
I'll rather dwell in my necessity.

ANTONIO

Why, fear not, man; I will not forfeit it:
Within these two months, that's a month before
This bond expires, I do expect return
Of thrice three times the value of this bond.

SHYLOCK

O father Abram, what these Christians are,
Whose own hard dealings teaches them suspect
The thoughts of others! Pray you, tell me this;
If he should break his day, what should I gain
By the exaction of the forfeiture?
A pound of man's flesh taken from a man
Is not so estimable, profitable neither,
As flesh of muttons, beefs, or goats. I say,
To buy his favour, I extend this friendship:
If he will take it, so; if not, adieu;
And, for my love, I pray you wrong me not.

ANTONIO

Yes Shylock, I will seal unto this bond.

SHYLOCK

Then meet me forthwith at the notary's;
Give him direction for this merry bond,
And I will go and purse the ducats straight,
See to my house, left in the fearful guard
Of an unthrifty knave, and presently
I will be with you.

ANTONIO

Hie thee, gentle Jew.

Exit Shylock

The Hebrew will turn Christian: he grows kind.

BASSANIO

I like not fair terms and a villain's mind.

ANTONIO

Come on: in this there can be no dismay;
My ships come home a month before the day.

Exeunt

(1467 words)

Unit 6

 **Notes**

1. This text is taken from *The Merchant of Venice* (Act 1, scene 3) by William Shakespeare, a play set in the 16th century. In the play a young merchant defaults on a large loan provided by Shylock, the Jewish moneylender. The loan is secured by the bond of a wealthy Christian merchant, Antonio.

2. William Shakespeare (26 April 1564 [baptised]—23 April 1616) was an English poet, playwright, and actor, widely regarded as the greatest writer in the English language and the world's pre-eminent dramatist. His extant works, including some collaborations, consist of about 37 plays, 154 sonnets, two long narrative poems, and a few other verses, of which the authorship of some is uncertain. His plays have been translated into every major living language and are performed more often than those of any other playwright.

Task 1 Questions for Comprehension and Discussion

Directions: Please answer the following questions.

1. Where does this scene take place? Why does Shakespeare select this setting for the play?
2. Who are the main characters in this scene? What kind of business are they involved in respectively?
3. How do Shylock and Antonio view each other?
4. What is the deal Shylock and Antonio agree on? Does Shylock charge Antonio interest on his loan? What can Shylock do if Antonio defaults on the loan and is unable to pay?

Task 2 Essay Writing

Directions: Next week you are going to join a seminar on the image of merchants in literature and you are invited to speak about The Merchant of Venice. Prepare a draft for your speech in 500 words in Chinese, using examples from the text above.

Unit 7

NATURE AND HUMAN SOCIETY

There can be no reason—except the selfish desire to preserve the privileges of the exploiting group—for refusing to extend the basic principle of equality of consideration to members of other species.

—Peter Singer

Learning Objectives

Upon the completion of this unit, you should be able to:

Remembering & Understanding	★ get a better understanding of the connection between nature and human society; ★ be aware of the historical and social background of the Animal Rights Movement;
Analyzing & Applying	★ write with better inductive reasoning; ★ identify unique perspectives and develop in-depth thinking; ★ make an effective refutation;
Evaluating & Creating	★ take a comparative approach to explore world literature; ★ develop points of comparison in cross-cultural communication.

Unit 7

Part One Lead-in

Section 1 Listening

Directions: Please fill in the blanks with words or sentences on the basis of what you have heard in the audio clip. Then discuss the following questions in pairs or groups.

English Lake District: Landscape and the Wild

The landscape of the English Lake District is, for a small block of hills, remarkably widely-known for its wildness and beauty. One recent July weekend, I walked with family and friends between the hills called St Sunday Crag and Fairfield. We had started from Patterdale in sunshine, with the long lake of Ullswater shining and blue, but the day had turned, and we were walking 1 _____, intermittently blasted by a cold wind and raindrops like steel shot. It was, by any standards, a wild scene. The rolling ridge was 2 _____ of loose rock, and we moved through a grey and 3 _____ of cloud. Suddenly the view to the south opened, 4 _____ two shining silver ribbons of water, Windermere and, further west, Coniston Water. The sky remained ominously black, but 5 _____ sun and dark shadow flowed over the lines of ridge and hill.

6. Do you know anything about the English Lake District? If yes, what is it famous for?
7. How did the speaker describe the changes in weather and scene during his walk with family and friends?
8. William Wordsworth and Norman Nicholson, the two poets and some of their lines about the Lake District are introduced. What is the core message these lines have conveyed to you? What is the point the speaker intended to make here?

Section 2 Watching

Directions: Please watch the video clip and discuss the following questions in pairs or groups.

Beethoven and His Pastoral Symphony

1. Why did Beethoven love to walk in the Austrian countryside?
2. What did music mean to Beethoven?
3. What were the titles of the first and second movements in his Sixth Symphony?
4. What was his source of inspiration for the Sixth Symphony?
5. How was the Sixth different from the other ones in terms of theme, mood or style?

Part Two Reading and Writing

Pre-Reading Questions

1. Do you have a pet?
2. Why is it popular for people to keep a pet?
3. Do you believe that animals also have feelings? If yes, what makes you believe so?

Text A

Preface to *Animal Liberation*[1]
(Excerpt)
Peter Singer[2]

1   The title of this book has a serious point behind it. A liberation movement is a demand for an end to prejudice and discrimination based on an arbitrary characteristic like race or sex. The classic instance is the Black Liberation movement. The immediate appeal of this movement, and its initial, if limited, success, *made it a model for* other oppressed groups. We soon became familiar with Gay Liberation and movements on behalf of American Indians and Spanish-speaking Americans. When a majority group—women—began their campaign some thought we had come to the end of the road. Discrimination on the basis of sex, it was said, was the last form of discrimination to be universally accepted and practiced without *secrecy* or pretense, even in those liberal circles that have long prided themselves on their freedom from prejudice against racial minorities.

2   We should always *be wary of* talking of "the last remaining form of discrimination." If we have learned anything from the liberation movements we should have learned how difficult it is to be aware of *latent* prejudices in our attitudes to particular groups until these prejudices are forcefully pointed out to us.

3   A liberation movement demands an expansion of our moral horizons. Practices that were previously regarded as natural and inevitable come to be seen as the result of an unjustifiable prejudice. Who can say with any confidence that none of his or her attitudes and practices can *legitimately* be questioned? If we wish to avoid being numbered among the oppressors, we must be prepared to rethink all our attitudes to other groups, including the most fundamental of them. We need to consider our attitudes from the point of view of those who suffer by them, and by the practices that follow from them. If we can *make* this unaccustomed *mental switch* we may discover a pattern in our attitudes and practices that operates so as consistently to benefit the same group—usually the group to which we ourselves belong—at the expense of another group. So we come to see that *there is a case for* a new liberation movement.

4   The aim of this book is to lead you to make this mental switch in your attitudes and practices toward a very large group of beings: members of species other than our own. I believe that our present attitudes to these beings are based on a long history of prejudice and arbitrary discrimination. I argue that there can be no reason—except the selfish desire to preserve the privileges of the exploiting group—for refusing to extend the basic principle of equality of consideration to members of other species. I ask you to recognize that your attitudes to members of other species are a form of prejudice no less objectionable than prejudice about a person's race or sex.

5   In comparison with other liberation movements, Animal Liberation has a lot of handicaps. First and most obvious is the fact that members of the exploited group cannot themselves make an organized protest against the treatment they receive (though they can and do protest to the best of their abilities individually). We have to *speak up* on behalf of those who cannot speak for themselves. You can appreciate how serious this handicap is by asking yourself how long blacks would have had to wait for equal rights if they had not been able to stand up for themselves and demand it. The less able a group is to stand up and organize against oppression, the more easily it is oppressed.

6   More significant still for the prospects of the Animal Liberation movement is the fact that almost all of the oppressing group are directly involved in, and see themselves as benefiting from, the oppression. There are few humans indeed who can view the oppression of animals with the *detachment* possessed, say, by Northern whites debating the institution of slavery in the Southern states of the Union. People who eat pieces of slaughtered nonhumans every day find it hard to imagine what else they could eat. On this issue, anyone who eats meat is an interested party. They benefit—or at least they think they benefit—from the present disregard of the interests of nonhuman animals. This makes persuasion more difficult. How many Southern slaveholders were persuaded by the arguments used by the Northern *abolitionists*, and accepted by nearly all of us today? Some, but not many. I can and do ask you to put aside your interest in eating meat when considering the arguments of this book; but I know from my own experience that with the best will in the world this is not an easy thing to do. For behind the mere momentary desire to eat meat on a particular occasion lie many years of habitual meat-eating which have conditioned our attitudes to animals.

7   Habit. That is the final barrier that the Animal Liberation movement faces. Habits not only of diet but also of thought and language must be challenged and altered. Habits of thought lead us to *brush aside* descriptions of cruelty to animals as emotional, for "animal-lovers only"; or if not that, then anyway the problem is so *trivial* in comparison to the problems of human beings that no sensible person could give it time and attention. This too is a prejudice—for how can one know that a problem is trivial until one has taken the time to examine its extent? Although in order to allow a more thorough treatment this book deals with only two of the many areas in which humans cause other animals to suffer, I do not think anyone who reads it to the end will ever again think that the only problems that *merit* time and energy are problems concerning humans.

8   The habits of thought that lead us to disregard the interests of animals can be challenged, as they are challenged in the following pages. This challenge has to be expressed in a language, which in this case happens to be English. The English language, like other languages, reflects the prejudices of its users. So authors who wish to challenge these prejudices are *in a* well-known type of *bind*: either they use

language that reinforces the very prejudices they wish to challenge, or else they fail to communicate with their audience. This book has already been forced along the former of these paths. We commonly use the word "animal" to mean "animals other than human beings." This usage sets humans apart from other animals, implying that we are not ourselves animals—an implication that everyone who has had elementary lessons in biology knows to be false.

9   In the popular mind the term "animal" *lumps together* beings as different as oysters and chimpanzees, while placing *a gulf* between chimpanzees and humans, although our relationship to those apes is much closer than the oyster's. Since there exists no other short term for the nonhuman animals, I have, in the title of this book and elsewhere in these pages, had to use "animal" as if it did not include the human animal. This is a regrettable *lapse* from the standards of revolutionary purity but it seems necessary for effective communication. Occasionally, however, to remind you that this is a matter of convenience only, I shall use longer, more accurate modes of referring to what was once called "the brute creation." In other cases, too, I have tried to avoid language which tends to *degrade* animals or disguise the nature of the food we eat.

(1257 words)

New Words

secrecy	[ˈsiːkrəsɪ]	n.	the trait of keeping things secret 秘密
latent	[ˈleɪtənt]	adj.	potentially existing but not presently evident or realized 潜伏的；隐藏的
legitimately	[lɪˈdʒɪtɪmɪtlɪ]	adv.	in a manner acceptable to common custom 合理地
detachment	[dɪˈtætʃmənt]	n.	avoiding emotional involvement 分离；超然
abolitionist	[ˌæbəʊˈlɪʃənɪst]	n.	a reformer who favors abolishing slavery 废奴主义者
trivial	[ˈtrɪvɪəl]	adj.	(*informal*) small and of little importance 不重要的
merit	[ˈmerɪt]	v.	be worthy or deserving 值得
lapse	[laps]	n.	a mistake resulting from inattention 失误
degrade	[ˈdɪˈgreɪd]	v.	reduce in worth or character, usually verbally 贬低

New Expressions

make it a model for	provide an example to copy 使之成为典型
be wary of	precaution against; guard against 提防；当心
make (a) mental switch	change in thinking 思想上作出改变

Unit 7

there is a case for sth.	give good arguments for doing something 有立论依据；有理由
speak up	speak one's opinion without fear or hesitation 无保留地说出
brush aside	refuse to consider it because you think it is not important or useful 置之不理
be in a bind	be in trouble 处于困境
lump together	(people or things) are considered as a group rather than separately 把……扯到一起；把……混为一谈
a gulf	an important or significant difference (between two people, things, or groups) 巨大的差距

Notes

1. The text was extracted from *Animal Liberation*, written by Australian philosopher Peter Singer, and published by New York Review/Random House in 1975. The book is widely considered within the animal liberation movement to be the founding philosophical statement of its ideas.

2. Peter Singer is an Australian moral philosopher. He is currently the Ira W. DeCamp Professor of Bioethics at Princeton University, and a Laureate Professor at the Centre for Applied Philosophy and Public Ethics at the University of Melbourne. He specializes in applied ethics and approaches ethical issues from a secular, utilitarian perspective. He is known in particular for *Animal Liberation*, a canonical text in animal rights/liberation theory.

Task 1 Generating the Outline

Directions: Please identify the thesis of the passage and the main point of each paragraph, and then find out how these points develop the thesis.

_____

_____

_____

_____

Task 2 Understanding the Text

Directions: Please answer the following questions based on Text A.

1. What common characters did the liberation movements mentioned in the first paragraph have?
2. Why did some people believe discrimination on the basis of sex was "the last form of discrimination"?
3. What rational argument for animal liberation did the author put forward?
4. What are the barriers facing the Animal Liberation movement the author identified in comparison with other liberation movements?
5. How did the author explain that the English language reflects prejudice towards nonhuman animals?

Task 3 Learning the Phrases

Directions: Please fill in the blanks in the sentences below with the phrases listed in the box. Change the forms if necessary.

> brush aside   there is a case   speak up   be wary of   be in a bind

1. _____ indeed for introducing a degree in the subject because of this fast changing world.
2. You should also _____ low-fat and fat-free foods (with the exception of dairy products), because food companies often compensate for the lack of fat by adding more sugar.
3. The leader needs to allow people to _____ but also to follow his lead.
4. Developing countries are particularly _____ because they aren't aware of how significant the problem can be.
5. But analysts at many American banks _____ such short-term worries.

Task 4 Translating the Sentences

Directions: Please translate the following sentences into Chinese.

1. Discrimination on the basis of sex, it was said, was the last form of discrimination to be universally accepted and practiced without secrecy or pretense, even in those liberal circles that have long prided themselves on their freedom from prejudice against racial minorities.

2. If we can make this unaccustomed mental switch we may discover a pattern in our attitudes and practices that operates so as consistently to benefit the same group—usually the group to which we ourselves belong—at the expense of another group.

3. I argue that there can be no reason—except the selfish desire to preserve the privileges of the exploiting group—for refusing to extend the basic principle of equality of consideration to members of other species.

4. There are few humans indeed who can view the oppression of animals with the detachment possessed, say, by Northern whites debating the institution of slavery in the Southern states of the

Union.

5. Habits of thought lead us to brush aside descriptions of cruelty to animals as emotional, for "animal-lovers only"; or if not that, then anyway the problem is so trivial in comparison to the problems of human beings that no sensible person could give it time and attention.

Task 5　Writing Exercises

Directions: Please answer the following questions according to your understanding of the text.

1. Reread the first three paragraphs of the text and discuss how the author persuaded the reader into seeing that there was a good argument for a new liberation movement, the Animal Liberation movement.

2. In what ways has the discussion of the Animal Liberation movement changed your view of animal interests and rights in everyday life?

Directions: Write a personal response in 300 words to one of the issues discussed in the text, using the rules of logical induction to build your argument. Be sure to write a topic sentence that helps the reader anticipate the organization of your written work.

Part Three Reading and Speaking

Pre-Reading Questions

1. In your opinion what might be reasons for the increasing popularity of the vegetarian diet worldwide?
2. Do you agree that the interests of human beings are far more important than those of animals?

Text B

We Have No Duty to Animals
Richard A. Posner

From: Richard A. Posner
To: Peter Singer

Dear Professor Singer:

1   I am impressed by your lucid and forceful argument for changing the ethical status of animals; and there is much in it with which I agree. I agree, for example, that human beings are not infinitely superior to or infinitely more valuable than other animals; indeed, I am prepared to drop "infinitely." I agree that we are animals and not *ensouled* demi-angels. I agree that *gratuitous* cruelty to and neglect of animals is wrong and that some costs should be incurred to reduce the suffering of animals raised for food or other human purposes or subjected to medical or other testing and experimentation.

2   But I do not agree that we have a duty to (the other) animals that arises from their being the equal members of a community composed of all those creatures in the universe that can feel pain, and that it is merely "prejudice" in a disreputable sense akin to racial prejudice or sexism that makes us "discriminate" in favor of our own species. You assume the existence of the universe-wide community of pain and demand reasons why the boundary of our concern should be drawn any more narrowly. I start from the bottom up, with the brute fact that we, like other animals, prefer our own—our own family, the "pack" that we happen to run with (being a social animal), and the larger *sodalities* constructed on the model of the smaller ones, of which the largest for most of us is our nation. Americans have distinctly less feeling for the pains and pleasures of foreigners than of other Americans and even less for most of the nonhuman animals that we share the world with.

3   Now you may reply that these are just facts about human nature; that they have no normative significance. But they do. Suppose a dog *menaced* a human infant and the only way to prevent the dog from biting the infant was to *inflict* severe pain on the

dog—more pain, in fact, than the bite would inflict on the infant. You would have to say, let the dog bite (for "if an animal feels pain, the pain matters as much as it does when a human feels pain," provided the pain is as great). But any normal person (and not merely the infant's parents!), including a philosopher when he is not self-consciously engaged in *philosophizing*, would say that it would be monstrous to spare the dog, even though to do so would minimize the sum of pain in the world.

4   I do not feel obliged to defend this reaction; it is a moral intuition deeper than any reason that could be given for it and *impervious* to any reason that you or anyone could give against it. Membership in the human species is not a "morally irrelevant fact," as the race and sex of human beings has come to seem. If the moral irrelevance of humanity is what philosophy teaches, and so we have to choose between philosophy and the intuition that says that membership in the human species is morally relevant, then it is philosophy that will have to go.

5   Toward the end of your statement you distinguish between pain and death and you acknowledge that the mental abilities of human beings may make their lives more valuable than those of animals. But this argument too is at war with our deepest intuitions. It implies that the life of a chimpanzee is more valuable than the life of a human being who, because he is profoundly retarded (though not comatose), has less mental ability than the chimpanzee. There are undoubtedly such cases. Indeed, there are people in the last stages of *Alzheimer's disease* who, though conscious, have less *mentation* than a dog. But killing such a person would be murder, while it is no crime at all to have a veterinarian kill one's pet dog because it has become *incontinent* with age. The logic of your position would require treating these killings alike. And if, for example, we could agree that although a normal human being's life is more valuable than a normal chimpanzee's life, it is only 100 times more valuable, you would have to concede that if a person had to choose between killing one human being and 101 chimpanzees, he should kill the human being. Against the deep *revulsion* that such results *engender* the concept of a transhuman community of sufferers beats its tinsel wings ineffectually.

6   What is needed to persuade us to alter our treatment of animals is not philosophy, let alone an atheistic philosophy (for one of the premises of your argument is that we have no souls) in a religious nation, but to learn to feel animals' pains as our pains and to learn that (if it is a fact, which I don't know) we can alleviate those pains without substantially reducing our standard of living and that of the rest of the world and without sacrificing medical and other scientific progress. Most of us, especially perhaps those of us who have lived with animals, have sufficient empathy for the suffering of animals to support the laws that forbid cruelty and neglect. We might go further if we knew more about animal feelings and about the existence of low-cost alternatives to pain-inflicting uses of animals. And so to expand and *invigorate* the laws that protect animals will require not philosophical arguments for reducing human beings to the level of the other animals but facts, facts that will stimulate a greater

empathetic response to animal suffering and facts that will alleviate concern about the human costs of further measures to reduce animal suffering.

(958 words)

New Words

ensoul	[ɪnˈsəʊl]	v.	to endow with a soul 赋予灵魂
gratuitous	[grəˈtjuːɪtəs]	adj.	unnecessary, and often harmful or upsetting; a formal word used showing disapproval 不必要的, 无缘无故的
sodality	[səʊˈdæləti]	n.	people engaged in a particular occupation 团体
menace	[ˈmenəs]	v.	pose a threat to; present a danger to 威胁
philosophize	[fɪˈlɒsəfaɪz]	v.	talk or think about important subjects, sometimes instead of doing something practical 理性地思考
impervious	[ɪmˈpɜːvɪəs]	adj.	not capable of being affected 不受影响的
mentation	[menˈteɪʃən]	n.	the process of using your mind to consider something carefully 精神活动
incontinent	[ɪnˈkɒntɪnənt]	adj.	not having control over urination and defecation 失控
revulsion	[rɪˈvʌlʃən]	n.	strong feeling of disgust or disapproval 厌恶
engender	[ɪnˈdʒendə]	v.	call forth 造成
invigorate	[ɪnˈvɪgəreɪt]	v.	impart vigor, strength, or vitality 使更有效、有活力

New Expressions

inflict on	impose something unpleasant 加痛苦于
Alzheimer's disease	a serious disease, especially affecting older people, that prevents the brain from functioning normally and causes loss of memory, loss of ability to speak clearly, etc. 阿尔茨海默症

Richard A. Posner is an American jurist, legal theorist, and economist. He is currently a judge on the United States Court of Appeals for the Seventh Circuit in Chicago and a Senior Lecturer at the University of Chicago Law School. He is a leading figure in the field of law and economics, and in 2000 was identified by *The Journal of Legal Studies* as the most cited legal scholar of the 20th century.

Posner engaged in a debate on the ethics of using animals in research with the philosopher Peter Singer in 2001 at *Slate* magazine. The text is one of a series of debate.

Task 1   Questions for Comprehension

Directions: Please answer the following questions based on Text B.

1. What was the common ground that Judge Posner and Professor Singer shared?
2. On what points did Judge Posner disagree with Professor Singer?
3. What are the suggestions proposed by Judge Posner to "alter our treatment of animals"?
4. How did Judge Posner develop his argument against Professor Singer's view?

Task 2   Questions for Discussion

Directions: Discuss the following questions in pairs or groups.

1. What do you think are effective ways to stimulate a greater empathetic response to animal suffering?
2. Some people believe that "empathy for pain and suffering of animals does not supersede advancing society." Please help come up with possible reasons for the statement. What makes them think that way?
3. Pick up one of the issues discussed in the two texts that really interests you. How would you respond to it? Take your position and use your personal experience to illustrate your points. Make a three-minute non-stop speech on Animal Liberation movement.

Part Four   Cross Cultural Communication

Passage A

醉翁亭记
（北宋）欧阳修

环滁皆山也。其西南诸峰，林壑尤美，望之蔚然而深秀者，琅琊也。山行六七里，渐闻水声潺潺而泻出于两峰之间者，酿泉也。峰回路转，有亭翼然临于泉上者，醉翁亭也。作亭者谁？山之僧曰智仙也。名之者谁？太守自谓也。太守与客来饮于此，饮少辄醉，而年又最高，故自号曰"醉翁"也。醉翁之意不在酒，在乎山水之间也。山水之乐，得之心而寓之酒也。

若夫日出而林霏开，云归而岩穴暝，晦明变化者，山间之朝暮也。野芳发而幽香，佳木秀而繁阴，风霜高洁，水落而石出者，山间之四时也。朝而往，暮而归，四时之景不同，而乐亦无穷也。

至于负者歌于途，行者休于树，前者呼，后者应，伛偻提携，往来而不绝者，滁人游也。临溪而渔，溪深而鱼肥，酿泉为酒，泉香而酒洌，山肴野蔌，杂然而前陈者，太守宴也。宴酣之乐，非丝非竹，射者中，弈者胜，觥筹交错，起坐而喧哗者，众宾欢也。苍颜白发，颓然乎其间者，太守醉也。

已而夕阳在山，人影散乱，太守归而宾客从也。树林阴翳，鸣声上下，游人去而禽鸟乐也。然而禽鸟知山林之乐，而不知人之乐；人知从太守游而乐，而不知太守之乐其乐也。醉能同其乐，醒能述以文者，太守也。太守谓谁？庐陵欧阳修也。

(479字)

 注 解

《醉翁亭记》是北宋文学家欧阳修创作的一篇散文。宋仁宗庆历五年(1045),参知政事范仲淹等人遭谗离职,欧阳修上书替他们分辩,被贬到滁州做了两年知州。《醉翁亭记》就写在这个时期。

文章描写了滁州一带朝暮四季自然景物不同的幽深秀美,滁州百姓和平宁静的生活,特别是作者在山林中与民一齐游赏宴饮的乐趣。

Task 1 Questions for Comprehension and Discussion

Directions: Please answer the following questions.

1. How did Ouyang Xiu develop and organize the main ideas in this great prose work of the Song Dynasty?
2. Apart from describing natural scenes and the parties, what might be the message or emotion do you think the author conveyed to the reader?
3. Make a list of three features of the article that have impressed you most. Explain each of them to the class.

Task 2 Summary

Directions: You would like to tell your international friends something about ancient Chinese literature next week. Write a summary of this masterpiece in 300 words in English.

_____

_____

_____

Passage B

Lines Composed a Few Miles Above Tintern Abbey[1], on Revisiting the Banks of the Wye[2] During a Tour

(Excerpt)

William Wordsworth[3]

Five years have past; five summers, with the length
Of five long winters! and again I hear
These waters, rolling from their mountain-springs
With a soft inland murmur. Once again
Do I behold these steep and lofty cliffs,
That on a wild secluded[4] scene impress
Thoughts of more deep seclusion; and connect
The landscape with the quiet of the sky.
The day is come when I again repose[5]
Here, under this dark sycamore[6], and view

These plots of cottage-ground, these orchard-tufts[7],
Which at this season, with their unripe fruits,
Are clad in[8] one green hue, and lose themselves
'Mid groves[9] and copses[10]. Once again I see
These hedge-rows, hardly hedge-rows[11], little lines
Of sportive wood run wild: these pastoral farms,
Green to the very door; and wreaths of smoke
Sent up, in silence, from among the trees!
With some uncertain notice, as might seem
Of vagrant[12] dwellers in the houseless woods,
Or of some Hermit's[13] cave, where by his fire
The Hermit sits alone.

These beauteous[14] forms,
Through a long absence, have not been to me
As is a landscape to a blind man's eye:
But oft, in lonely rooms, and 'mid the din[15]
Of towns and cities, I have owed to them
In hours of weariness, sensations sweet,
Felt in the blood, and felt along the heart;
And passing even into my purer mind,
With tranquil restoration: feelings too
Of unremembered pleasure: such, perhaps,
As have no slight or trivial influence
On that best portion of a good man's life,
His little, nameless, unremembered, acts
Of kindness and of love. Nor less, I trust,
To them I may have owed another gift,
Of aspect more sublime[16]; that blessed mood,
In which the burthen[17] of the mystery,
In which the heavy and the weary weight
Of all this unintelligible world,
Is lightened: that serene[18] and blessed mood,
In which the affections gently lead us on,
Until, the breath of this corporeal[19] frame
And even the motion of our human blood
Almost suspended, we are laid asleep
In body, and become a living soul:
While with an eye made quiet by the power
Of harmony, and the deep power of joy,
We see into the life of things.

If this
Be but a vain belief, yet, oh! how oft
In darkness and amid the many shapes
Of joyless daylight; when the fretful[20] stir
Unprofitable, and the fever of the world,
Have hung upon the beatings of my heart
How oft, in spirit, have I turned to thee,
O sylvan Wye! thou wanderer thro' the woods,
How often has my spirit turned to thee!

And now, with gleams of half-extinguished thought,
With many recognitions dim and faint,
And somewhat of a sad perplexity,
The picture of the mind revives again:
While here I stand, not only with the sense
Of present pleasure, but with pleasing thoughts
That in this moment there is life and food
For future years. And so I dare to hope,
Though changed, no doubt, from what I was when first
I came among these hills; when like a roe[21]
I bounded o'er the mountains, by the sides
Of the deep rivers, and the lonely streams,
Wherever nature led: more like a man
Flying from something that he dreads, than one
Who sought the thing he loved. For nature then
(The coarser[22] pleasures of my boyish days,
And their glad animal movements all gone by)
To me was all in all. I cannot paint
What then I was. The sounding cataract[23]
Haunted me like a passion: the tall rock,
The mountain, and the deep and gloomy wood,
Their colours and their forms, were then to me
An appetite; a feeling and a love,
That had no need of a remoter charm,
By thought supplied, nor any interest
Unborrowed from the eye. That time is past,
And all its aching joys are now no more,
And all its dizzy raptures[24]. Not for this
Faint I, nor mourn nor murmur, other gifts
Have followed; for such loss, I would believe,
Abundant recompense. For I have learned

To look on nature, not as in the hour
Of thoughtless youth; but hearing oftentimes
The still, sad music of humanity,
Nor harsh nor grating[25], though of ample power
To chasten[26] and subdue[27]. And I have felt
A presence that disturbs me with the joy
Of elevated thoughts; a sense sublime
Of something far more deeply interfused,
Whose dwelling is the light of setting suns,
And the round ocean and the living air,
And the blue sky, and in the mind of man;
A motion and a spirit, that impels
All thinking things, all objects of all thought,
And rolls through all things. Therefore am I still
A lover of the meadows and the woods,
And mountains; and of all that we behold
From this green earth; of all the mighty world
Of eye, and ear, both what they half create,
And what perceive; well pleased to recognize
In nature and the language of the sense,
The anchor of my purest thoughts, the nurse,
The guide, the guardian of my heart, and soul
Of all my moral being.

(885 words)

Notes

1. Tintern Abbey: a beautiful ruined abbey by the River Wye, near the border between England and Wales. It was originally built in the 12th century. It has been painted by many artists, including Turner (1775—1851, a major English artist, famous for his landscape and seascape paintings), and Wordsworth wrote a romantic poem about it in his *Lyrical Ballads. Tintern Abbey* was one of the pieces.
2. Wye [waɪ]: a river which rises in the mountains of western Wales and flows 208 km generally south-eastwards, entering the Seven Estuary at Chepstow. In its lower reaches it forms part of the border between Wales and England.
3. Williams Wordsworth (1770—1850): one of the most popular of all English poets who, together with Samuel Taylor Coleridge, started the Romantic Movement in English poetry. His poems are mainly about the beauty of nature and its relationship with all human beings. Many of them describe the countryside of the Lake District in north-west England, where he was born and spent most of his life. His best-known works include *Lyrical Ballads* (1798), a collection of poems by himself and Coleridge, *Poems* (1807), and *The Prelude* (1850).

4. secluded: hidden from general view or use
5. repose: to rest
6. sycamore: 槭树
7. tuft: a bunch of growing grass
8. clad in: covered in a particular thing
9. grove: a small growth of trees without underbrush
10. copse: a dense growth of bushes
11. hedge-rows: a fence formed by a row of closely planted shrubs or bushes
12. vagrant: someone has no established residence
13. Hermit: one retired from society for religious reasons
14. beauteous: (*poetic*) beautiful, especially to the sight
15. din: a loud harsh or strident noise
16. Of aspect more sublime: of a more sublime nature
17. burthen: a variant of "burden"
18. serene: completely clear and fine
19. corporeal: physical rather than spiritual
20. fretful: unhappy or uncomfortable
21. roe: fish eggs
22. coarse: not smooth or soft; rough
23. cataract: a large waterfall; violent rush of water over a precipice
24. rapture: a state of being carried away by overwhelming emotion
25. grating: unpleasantly harsh in sound
26. chasten: correct by punishment or discipline
27. subdue: put down by force or intimidation

Task 1　Questions for Comprehension and Discussion

Directions: Please answer the following questions.

1. How did nature inspire the poet for his literary work?
2. In what aspects is W. Wordsworth's poem different from and similar to Ouyang Xiu's piece.

Task 2　Summary

Directions: Your friend Mark from England would like to work with you on a project of comparative literature. You two decided to play a language shifting game, that is, Mark had to explain Ouyang Xiu's prose in English, and you Wordsworth's piece in Chinese. Please get yourself prepared by writing a summary in Chinese of Lines Composed a Few Miles Above Tintern Abbey in 500 characters.

Unit 8

TECHNOLOGY AND ETHICS

As the amount of data expands exponentially, nearly all of it carries someone's digital fingerprints.

—*Patrick Tucker*

Learning Objectives

Upon the completion of this unit, you should be able to:

Remembering & Understanding	★ be aware of the benefits and disadvantages of technology; ★ renew your understanding of privacy in the age of big data;
Analyzing & Applying	★ weigh privacy against convenience; ★ balance privacy against public interests;
Evaluating & Creating	★ give advice on how to secure our privacy; ★ prepare a speech draft on the history of technology in China.

Part One Lead-in

Section 1 Listening

Directions: Please fill in the blanks with words or sentences on the basis of what you have heard in the audio clip. Then discuss the questions in pairs or groups.

Epidemic Disease: Is the Internet Our Key to Survival?

   Well that was the real misstep 1 _____ density. It 2 _____ that the Native Americans in a show of good will, they would gather in the tents of people who 3 _____ smallpox, everyone would gather together and again unfortunately that was a gesture that was sort of ill fated.

   This is exactly the fear that all major medical centers have the next time we have a new strain hitting us, whether it's the Asian flu or Swine flu 4 _____, the big fear that medical centers have is that everybody with a cough is going to come flocking into the medical center to get 5_____ _____. This is really dangerous.

6. What is the speaker's answer to the question: Is the Internet Our Key to Survival? What are his reasons?
7. How did people respond to the black plague in Europe? What would the Native Americans do in the face of smallpox? What does the speaker want to say with these examples?
8. According to the speaker, why are the telepresence and the telemedicine very useful in our response to epidemic diseases?
9. How does the Center for Disease Control track the flu? How about Google? Which one is more efficient?

Section 2 Watching

Directions: Please watch the video clip and discuss the following questions in pairs or groups.

The Truman Show: The Interview

1. Have you watched any reality shows before? In what ways are they similar to or different from The Truman Show? Why do you think people love to watch reality shows?
2. How was Truman selected to be on the show? Where did he live? What was his childhood dream and what was he told?
3. How does Christof—the director of the Truman Show—regard his own privacy? What does this reveal?
4. How have cameras changed our lives? What should we do to make good use of them?

Unit 8

Part Two Reading and Writing

Pre-Reading Questions

1. To process huge amount of data is often referred to as "data mining", comparing big data to mines. In what ways do you think big data are mines?
2. Have you ever heard of stories of privacy violation? Share them in groups of four.

Text A

Has Big Data Made Anonymity Impossible?[1]
Patrick Tucker[2]

As the amount of data expands exponentially, nearly all of it carries someone's digital fingerprints.

1   In 1995, the European Union introduced privacy legislation that defined "personal data" as any information that could identify a person, directly or indirectly. The legislators were apparently thinking of things like documents with an identification number, and they wanted them protected just as if they carried your name.

2   Today, that definition encompasses far more information than those European legislators could ever have imagined—easily more than all the *bits* and *bytes* in the entire world when they wrote their law 18 years ago.

3   Here's what happened. First, the amount of data created each year has grown *exponentially*: it reached 2.8 zettabytes in 2012, a number that's as *gigantic* as it sounds, and will double again by 2015, according to the *consultancy* IDC. Of that, about three-quarters is generated by individuals as they create and move digital files. A typical American office worker produces 1.8 million *megabytes* of data each year. That is about 5,000 megabytes a day, including downloaded movies, Word files, e-mail, and the bits generated by computers as that information is moved along mobile networks or across the Internet.

4   Much of this data is invisible to people and seems impersonal. But it's not. What modern data science is finding is that nearly any type of data can be used, much like a fingerprint, to identify the person who created it: your choice of movies on Netflix, the location signals *emitted* by your cell phone, even your pattern of walking as recorded by a *surveillance* camera. *In effect*, the more data there is, the less any of it can be said to be private, since the richness of that data makes *pinpointing* people "*algorithmically* possible," says Princeton University computer scientist Arvind Narayanan.

5   We're well down this path already. The types of information we've thought of as personal data in the past—our name, address, or credit card records—are already bought and sold by data *brokers* like Acxiom, a company that holds an average of 1,500

pieces of information on more than 500 million consumers around the world. This was data that people put into the public domain on a survey form or when they *signed up for* services such as TiVo.

6   Acxiom uses information about the make and year of your car, your income and investments, and your age, education, and zip code to place you into one of 70 different "PersonicX" clusters, which are "summarized indicators of lifestyle, interests and activities." Did you just finalize a divorce or become an *empty nester*? Such "life events," which move people from one consumer class to another, are of key interest to Acxiom and its advertising clients. The company says it can analyze its data to predict 3,000 different *propensities*, such as how a person may respond to one brand over another.

7   Yet these data brokers today are considered somewhat old-fashioned compared with Internet companies like Facebook, which have automated the collection of personal information so it can be done *in real time*. According to its financial filings at the time of its *IPO*, Facebook stores around 111 megabytes of photos and videos for each of its users, who now number more than a billion. That's 100 petabytes of personal information right there. In some European legal cases, *plaintiffs* have learned that Facebook's records of their interactions with the site—including text messages, things they "liked," and addresses of computers they used—run to 800 printed pages, *adding up to* another few megabytes per user.

8   In a step that's worrisome to digital-privacy advocates, offline and online data sets are now being connected to help marketers target advertisements more precisely. In February, Facebook announced a deal with Acxiom and other data brokers to *merge* their data, linking real-world activities to those on the Web. At a March investor meeting, Acxiom's chief science officer claimed that its data could now be linked to 90 percent of U.S. social profiles.

9   Such data sets are often portrayed as having been "anonymized" in some way, but the more data they involve, the less likely that is to be actually true. Mobile-phone companies, for instance, record users' locations, strip out the phone numbers, and sell *aggregate* data sets to merchants or others interested in people's movements (see "How Wireless Carriers Are Monetizing Your Movements"). MIT researchers Yves-Alexandre de Montjoye and César A. Hidalgo have shown that even when such location data is anonymous, just four different data points about a phone's position can usually link the phone to a unique person.

10   The greater the amount of personal data that becomes available, the more informative the data gets. In fact, with enough data, it's even possible to discover information about a person's future. Last year Adam Sadilek, a University of Rochester researcher, and John Krumm, an engineer at Microsoft's research lab, showed they could predict a person's approximate location up to 80 weeks into the future, at an accuracy of above 80 percent. To get there, the pair mined what they described as a "massive data set" collecting 32,000 days of GPS readings taken from 307 people and 396 vehicles.

Unit 8

They then imagined the commercial applications, like ads that say "Need a haircut? In four days, you will be within 100 meters of a salon that will have a $5 special at that time."

Sadilek and Krumm called their system "*Far Out*." That's a pretty good description of where personal data is taking us.

(911 words)

New Words

anonymity	[ˌænəˈnɪmətɪ]	*n.*	the state of having no known name or identity or known source 匿名
bit	[bɪt]	*n.*	the smallest unit of information that is held in a computer's memory 比特 (计算机存储的最小信息单位)
byte	[baɪt]	*n.*	a unit of storage approximately equivalent to one printed character 字节
exponentially	[ˌɛkspəˈnɛnʃəlɪ]	*adv.*	(increase) more and more very rapidly 以指数方式(增长)
gigantic	[dʒaɪˈgæntɪk]	*adj.*	extremely large in size, amount, or degree 巨大的
consultancy	[kənˈsʌltənsɪ]	*n.*	a company that gives expert advice on a particular subject 咨询公司
megabyte	[ˈmɛgəˌbaɪt]	*n.*	one million bytes of data 兆字节
emit	[ɪˈmɪt]	*v.*	produce and send 发出
surveillance	[sɜːˈveɪləns]	*n.*	the careful watching of someone, especially by an organization such as the police or the army 监视
pinpoint	[ˈpɪnˌpɔɪnt]	*v.*	discover or show exactly where somebody or something is 给……准确定位
algorithmically	[ˌælgəˈrɪðmɪklɪ]	*adv.*	of or relating to or having the characteristics of an algorithm 算法地
broker	[ˈbrəʊkə]	*n.*	a person whose job is to buy and sell securities, foreign money, real estate, or goods for other people 经纪人, 掮客
propensity	[prəˈpɛnsɪtɪ]	*n.*	a natural tendency to behave in a particular way (行为) 倾向
plaintiff	[ˈpleɪntɪf]	*n.*	a person who brings a case against another person in a court of law 原告
merge	[mɜːdʒ]	*v.*	combine or come together to make one whole thing (使)合并;(使)融合
aggregate	[ˈægrɪgɪt]	*adj.*	made up of several amounts that are added together to form a total number 总数的,总计的

New Expressions

in effect	in reality 事实上
sign up for	to agree to join or use something 参加或使用
empty nester	a parent whose children have grown up and left home 空巢老人
in real time	without delay or hesitation 实时地
IPO	Initial Public Offering 首次公开募股
add up to	result in (a total) when separate amounts are put together 总计为
far out	very strange or extreme 异乎寻常的

1. This text is an article from *MIT Technology Review* in 2013.
2. Patrick Tucker, the author of the text, is the technology editor of *Defense One* and the author of the book, *The Naked Future: What Happens in a World That Anticipates Your Every Move* (2014).

Task 1 Generating the Outline

Directions: Please identify the thesis of the passage and the main point of each paragraph, and then find out how these points develop the thesis.

_____
_____
_____
_____
_____
_____
_____
_____
_____
_____

Task 2 Understanding the Text

Directions: Please answer the following questions based on Text A.

1. What kind of data is "personal"? What kind of data is "impersonal"?
2. What do companies such as Facebook and Acxiom do with data? Why is it worrisome to digital-privacy advocates when these companies are going to merge their data?
3. According to the author, is it effective to "anonymize" data sets? Why?
4. Read the haircut advertisement in Para. 11 again and come up with your own example.
5. What is the author's answer to the question in the title? What is your answer to it?

Unit 8

Task 3 Learning the Phrases

Directions: Please fill in the blanks in the sentences below with the phrases listed in the box. Change the forms if necessary.

> in effect   sign up for   in real time   add up to   far out

1. That $50 a month leaving your bank account on payday that you barely notice will _____ $600 a year.
2. Some of the ideas for putting that computing power to work were pretty _____.
3. _____, journalists not only observe the event they're reporting about, they're also absorbing it.
4. You can now use your phone to translate speech _____, having a conversation that would not have been possible in the past.
5. You want users to _____ your service, so make it as easy for them as possible.

Task 4 Translating the Sentences

Directions: Please translate the following sentences into Chinese.

1. The legislators were apparently thinking of things like documents with an identification number, and they wanted them protected just as if they carried your name.

2. Much of this data is invisible to people and seems impersonal. But it's not.

3. In a step that's worrisome to digital-privacy advocates, offline and online data sets are now being connected to help marketers target advertisements more precisely.

4. The greater the amount of personal data that becomes available, the more informative the data gets.

5. Need a haircut? In four days, you will be within 100 meters of a salon that will have a $5 special at that time.

Task 5 Writing Exercises

Directions: Please answer the following questions according to your understanding of the text.

Do you think privacy can be compromised for convenience? Why? Write a 300-word essay on this topic.

Directions: What are the major privacy legislations around the world? Carry out a small research and summarize your findings in 300 words.

Part Three Reading and Speaking

Pre-Reading Questions

1. To use an online service or a software, users are usually requested to either "agree and continue" or quit after reading the "notice and consent". What are these terms of use about? Do you usually read them closely as requested? Why or why not?
2. Imagine you are writing for a special section on your university website: "What are the best ways to protect your privacy?" Choose one topic from below or come up with a topic of your own. Then list at least five suggestions for your fellow students.
   a. What are the best ways to protect your privacy when you chat online?
   b. What are the best ways to protect your privacy when you use smart phones?
   c. What are the best ways to protect your privacy when you shop online?

Text B

From Privacy to Accountability[1]

Viktor Mayer-Schönberger[2] and Kenneth Cukier[3]

1   For decades an essential principle of privacy laws around the world has been to put individuals in control by letting them decide whether, how, and by whom their personal information may be processed. In the Internet age, this *laudable* ideal has often *morphed into* a *formulaic* system of "notice and consent." In the era of big data, however, when much of data's value is in secondary uses that may have been unimagined when the data was collected, such a mechanism to ensure privacy is no longer suitable.

2   We *envision* a very different privacy framework for the big-data age, one focused less on individual consent at the time of collection and more on holding data users accountable for what they do. In such a world, firms will formally assess a particular reuse of data based on the impact it has on individuals whose personal information is being processed. This does not have to be *onerously* detailed in all cases, as future privacy laws will define broad categories of uses, including ones that are permissible without or with only limited, standardized *safeguards*. For riskier initiatives, regulators will establish *ground rules* for how data users should assess the dangers of a planned use and determine what best avoids or *mitigates* potential harm. This *spurs* creative reuses of the data, while at the same time it ensures that sufficient measures are taken to see that individuals are not hurt.

3   Running a formal big-data use assessment correctly and implementing its findings accurately offers *tangible* benefits to data users: they will be free to pursue secondary uses of personal data in many instances without having to go back to individuals to get their explicit consent. On the other hand, *sloppy* assessments or poor implementation of safeguards will expose data users to *legal liability*, and regulatory actions such as mandates, fines, and perhaps even criminal prosecution. Data-user accountability only works when it has teeth.

4   To see how this could happen in practice, take the example of the datafication of *posteriors*. Imagine that a company sold a car antitheft service which used a driver's sitting posture as a unique identifier. Then, it later reanalyzed the information to predict drivers' "attention states," such as whether they were *drowsy* or *tipsy* or angry, in order to send alerts to other drivers nearby to prevent accidents. Under today's privacy rules, the firm might believe it needed a new round of notice and consent because it hadn't previously received permission to use the information in this way. But under a system of data-user accountability, the company would assess the dangers of the intended use, and if it found them minimal it could just go ahead with its plan—and improve road safety in the process.

5   Shifting the burden of responsibility from the public to the users of data makes

sense for a number of reasons. They know much more than anybody else, and certainly more than consumers or regulators, about how they intend to use the data. By conducting the assessment themselves (or hiring experts to do it) they will avoid the problem of revealing confidential business strategies to outsiders. Perhaps most important, the data users *reap* most of the benefits of secondary use, so it's only fair to hold them accountable for their actions and place the burden for this review on them.

6   With such an alternative privacy framework, data users will no longer be legally required to delete personal information once it has served its primary purpose, as most privacy laws currently demand. This is an important change, since, as we've seen, only by *tapping* the *latent* value of data can latter-day Maurys flourish by *wringing* the most value *out of* it for their own—and society's— benefit. Instead, data users will be allowed to keep personal information longer, though not forever. Society needs to carefully weigh the rewards from reuse against the risks from too much *disclosure*.

7   To strike the appropriate balance, regulators may choose different time frames for reuse, depending on the data's *inherent* risk, as well as on different societies' values. Some nations may be more cautious than others, just as some sorts of data may be considered more sensitive than others. This approach also *banishes* the *specter* of "permanent memory"—the risk that one can never escape one's past because the digital records can always be *dredged up*. Otherwise our personal data *hovers* over us like the *Sword of Damocles*, threatening to *impale* us years hence with some private detail or regrettable purchase. Time limits also create an incentive for data holders to use it before they lose it. This strikes what we believe is a better balance for the big-data era: firms get the right to use personal data longer, but in return they have to take on responsibility for its uses as well as the obligation to erase personal data after a certain period of time.

8   In addition to a regulatory shift from "privacy by consent" to "privacy through accountability," we envision technical innovation to help protect privacy in certain instances. One *nascent* approach is the concept of "*differential* privacy": deliberately *blurring* the data so that a *query* of a large dataset doesn't reveal exact results but only approximate ones. This makes it difficult and costly to associate particular data points with particular people.

9   *Fuzzing* the information sounds as if it might destroy valuable insights. But it need not—or at least, the tradeoff can be favorable. For instance, experts in technology policy note that Facebook relies on a form of differential privacy when it reports information about its users to potential advertisers: the numbers it reports are approximate, so they can't help reveal individual identities. Looking up Asian women in Atlanta who are interested in Ashtanga yoga(阿斯汤加瑜伽)will produce a result such as "about 400" rather than an exact number, making it impossible to use the information to narrow down statistically on someone specific.

10   The shift in controls from individual consent to data-user accountability is a

Unit 8

fundamental and essential change necessary for effective big-data governance. But it is not the only one.

(*1015 words*)

New Words

accountability	[ə͵kaʊntəˈbɪləti]	*n.*	responsibility to somebody, or for some activity 责任
laudable	[ˈlɔːdəbəl]	*a.*	deserving to be praised or admired 可嘉许的,值得赞美的
formulaic	[͵fɔːmjʊˈleɪɪk]	*adj.*	not original, used many times before in similar situations 公式化的
envision	[ɪnˈvɪʒən]	*v.*	imagine 设想
onerously	[ˈɒnərəsli]	*adv.*	difficultly or unpleasantly 繁重地;费力地
safeguard	[ˈseɪfˌɡɑːd]	*n.*	a law, rule, or measure intended to prevent somebody or something from being harmed 安全条例;防护措施
mitigate	[ˈmɪtɪˌɡeɪt]	*v.*	make something less unpleasant, serious, or painful 缓解
spur	[spɜː]	*v.*	makes it happen faster or sooner 使更快发生,加速
tangible	[ˈtændʒəbəl]	*adj.*	clear enough or definite enough to be easily seen, felt, or noticed 清晰明确的
sloppy	[ˈslɒpi]	*adj.*	If you describe someone's work or activities as sloppy, you mean they have been done in a careless and lazy way. 慵懒的,马虎的
posterior	[pɒˈstɪərɪə]	*n.*	buttocks 臀部
drowsy	[ˈdraʊzi]	*adj.*	sleepy and not able to think clearly 昏昏欲睡的
tipsy	[ˈtɪpsi]	*adj.*	slightly drunk 微醺的
reap	[riːp]	*v.*	If you reap the benefits or the rewards of something, you enjoy the good things that happen as a result of it. 获得
tap	[tæp]	*v.*	make good use of 利用
latent	[ˈleɪtənt]	*adj.*	hidden and not obvious at the moment, but which may develop further in the future 潜在的
disclosure	[dɪsˈkləʊʒə]	*n.*	the act of giving people new or secret information 公开
inherent	[ɪnˈhɪrənt]	*adj.*	existing in something as a permanent, essential, or characteristic attribute 内在的
banish	[ˈbænɪʃ]	*v.*	get rid of 消除
specter	[ˈspɛktə]	*n.*	a ghostly appearing figure 幽灵
hover	[ˈhɒvə]	*v.*	stay in the same position in the air 悬空
impale	[ɪmˈpeɪl]	*v.*	pierce or transfix with a sharp instrument 刺穿
nascent	[ˈnæsənt]	*n.*	Nascent things or processes are just beginning, and are expected to become stronger or to grow bigger. 新生的;初期的

differential	[ˌdɪfəˈrenʃl]	*adj.*	of, showing, or depending on a difference 差别的, 有区别的
blur	[blɜː]	*v.*	make unclear 使……模糊不清
query	[ˈkwɪərɪ]	*n.*	a question, especially one that you ask an organization, publication, or expert 疑问
fuzz	[fʌz]	*v.*	to make or become indistinct; blur 使……变模糊

morph into	change into something very different 转变成
ground rule	basic principles on which future action will be based 基本原则
legal liability	the legal bound obligation to pay debts 法律责任
wring out of	When you wring out a wet cloth or a wet piece of clothing, you squeeze the water out of it by twisting it strongly. 拧干, 榨取
dredge up	mention something unpleasant from the past 回忆起
Sword of Damocles	constant threat; imminent peril 达摩克利斯剑, 喻指临头的危险

1. The text is an excerpt from the book, *Big Data: A Revolution That Will Transform How We Live, Work and Think* (2013) by Viktor Mayer-Schönberger and Kenneth Cukier.
2. Viktor Mayer-Schönberger, a co-author of the text, is Professor of Internet Governance and Regulation at the Oxford Internet Institute, University of Oxford.
3. Kenneth Cukier, a co-author of the text, is the Data Editor of *The Economist*.

Task 1 Questions for Comprehension

Directions: Please answer the following questions based on Text B.

1. What were the approaches towards privacy protection before and during the Internet age? What is the privacy framework the authors envision for the era of big data?
2. What do the authors mean by "Data-user accountability only works when it has teeth." at the end of Para. 3?
3. How long should data users be allowed to keep personal information? Why does it matter?
4. What is a "differential privacy"?
5. According to the authors, data-user accountability is not the only change necessary for effective big-data governance (Para. 10). Can you think of some other examples in this regard?

Task 2 Questions for Discussion

Directions: Divide the class into groups of four. In each group, two students argue for and the others against the motion "society benefits when we share personal information online." The proposition team and the opposition team take turns to give speeches, each of which should be within five minutes.

Part Four　Cross Cultural Communication

Passage A

《劝学篇》序[1]
（节选）
张之洞[2]

昔楚庄王之霸也，以民生在勤箴其民，以日讨军实儆其军，以祸至无日训其国人。夫楚当春秋鲁文、宣之际，土方辟，兵方强，国势方张，齐、晋、秦、宋无敢抗颜行，谁能祸楚者？何为而急迫震惧，如是之皇皇耶？君子曰："不知其祸，则辱至矣；知其祸，则福至矣。"今日之世变，岂特春秋所未有，抑秦、汉以至元、明所未有也。语其祸，则共工之狂，辛有之痛，不足喻也。

庙堂旰食，乾惕震厉，方将改弦以调琴瑟，异等以储将相，学堂建，特科设，海内志士发愤搤捥。於是图救时者言新学，虑害道者守旧学，莫衷於一。旧者因噎而食废，新者歧多而羊亡。旧者不知通，新者不知本。不知通则无应敌制变之术，不知本则有非薄名教之心。夫如是，则旧者愈病新，新者愈厌旧，交相为瘉，而恢诡倾危、乱名改作之流，遂杂出其说，以荡众心。学者摇摇，中无所主，邪说暴行，植流天下。敌既至，无与战，敌未至，无与安，吾恐中国之祸，不在四海之外，而在九州之内矣。

窃维古来世运之明晦，人才之盛衰，其表在政，其里在学。不佞承乏两湖，与有教士化民之责，夙夜兢兢，思有所以裨助之者。乃规时势，综本末，著论二十四篇，以告两湖之士，海内君子，与我同志，亦所不隐。内篇务本以正人心，外篇务通以开风气。

……

二十四篇之义，括之以五知：一知耻，耻不如日本，耻不如土耳其，耻不如暹罗，耻不如古巴。二知惧，惧为印度，惧为越南、缅甸、朝鲜，惧为埃及，惧为波兰。三知变，不变其习，不能变法，不变其法，不能变器。四知要，中学考古非要，致用为要；西学亦有别，西艺非要，西政为要。五知本，在海外不忘国，见异俗不忘亲，多智巧不忘圣。凡此所说，窃尝考诸中庸而有合焉。鲁，弱国也，哀公问政，而孔子告之曰："好学近乎知，力行近乎仁，知耻近乎勇。"终之曰："果能此道矣，虽愚必明，虽柔必强。"兹内篇所言，皆求仁之事也；外篇所言，皆求智求勇之事也。

夫中庸之书，岂特原心眇忽校理分寸而已哉！孔子以鲁秉礼而积弱，齐、邾、吴、越皆得以兵侮之，故为此言，以破鲁国臣民之聋聩，起鲁国诸懦之废疾，望鲁国幡然有为，以复文武之盛。然则无学、无力、无耻，则愚且柔，有学、有力、有耻，则明且强。在鲁且然，况以七十万方里之广，四百兆人民之众者哉！吾恐海内士大夫狃於晏安，而不知祸之将及也，故举楚事；吾又恐甘於暴弃，而不复求强也，故举鲁事。易曰："其亡，其亡，系於苞桑。"惟知亡，则知强矣。光绪二十四年三月南皮张之洞书。

(963字)

1. 本篇节选自张之洞《劝学篇》序。主张"中学为体，西学为用"。即教育首先要传授中国传统的经史之学，这是一切学问的基础，要放在率先的地位，然后再学习西学中有用的东西，以补中学的不足。
2. 张之洞，清代洋务派代表人物之一，与曾国藩、李鸿章、左宗棠并称晚清"四大名臣"。

Task 1 Questions for Comprehension and Discussion

Directions: Please answer the following questions.

1. What happened in China when Zhang Zhidong wrote this article in 1898? According to the author, what are the reasons behind the social changes?
2. What is the purpose of the writing?
3. What are the five crucial things to know（五知）?
4. Why does the author quote Confucius as saying "好学近乎知，力行近乎仁，知耻近乎勇。"?

Task 2 Essay Writing

Directions: Recently your British friend Hillary got very interested in modern Chinese history and sent you the excerpt above from Exhortation to Study, which she found quite difficult to understand. Write an email in 300 words in English to help Hillary understand the main ideas of the text.

Passage B

Precursors of Modern Science

Joseph Needham

The extraordinary inventiveness, and insight into nature, of ancient and medieval China raises two fundamental questions. First, why should the Chinese have been so far in advance of other civilizations; and second, why aren't they now centuries ahead of the rest of the world? We think it was a matter of the very different social and economic systems in China and the West. Modern science arose only in Europe in the seventeenth century when the best method of discovery was itself discovered; but the discoveries and inventions made then and thereafter depended in so many cases on centuries of previous Chinese progress in science, technology and medicine.

The English philosopher Francis Bacon (1561—1626) selected three inventions, paper and printing, gunpowder, and the magnetic compass, which had done more, he thought, than any religious conviction, or any astrological influence, or any conqueror's achievements, to transform completely the modern world and mark it off from Antiquity and the Middle Ages. He regarded the origins of these inventions as "obscure and inglorious" and he died without ever knowing that all of them were Chinese. We have done our best to put this record straight.

Chauvinistic Westerners, of course, always try to minimize the indebtedness of Europe to China in Antiquity and the Middle Ages, but often the circumstantial evidence is compelling. For example the first blast furnaces for cast iron, now known to be Scandinavian of the late eighth century AD, are of closely similar form to those of the previous century in China; while as late as the seventeenth century all the magnetic compasses of surveyors and astronomers pointed south, not north, just as the compasses of China had always done. In many cases, however, we cannot as yet detect the capillary channels through which knowledge was conveyed from East to West. Nevertheless we have always adopted the very reasonable assumption that the longer the time elapsing between the appearance of a discovery or invention in one part of the world, and its appearance later on in some other part of the world far away, the less likely is it that the new thing was independently invented or discovered.

But all these things being agreed, a formidable question then presents itself. If the Chinese were so advanced in Antiquity and the Middle Ages, how was it that the Scientific Revolution, the coming of modem science into the world, happened only in Europe?

The fact is that in the seventeenth century we have to face a package deal; the Scientific Revolution was accompanied both by the Protestant Reformation and by the rise of capitalism, the ascendancy of the entrepreneurial bourgeoisie. Distinctively modem science, which then developed, was a mathematization of hypotheses about nature, combined with relentless experimentation. The sciences of all the ancient and medieval worlds had had an indelibly ethnic stamp but now nature was addressed for the first time in a universal and international language, the precise and quantitative idiom of mathematics, a tongue which every man and woman, irrespective of colour, creed or race, can use and master if given the proper training. And to the technique of experiment the same applies. It was like the merchant's universal standard of value. How one looks at the primary causative factor in all this depends on one's own background. If one is a theologian one probably thinks that the liberation of the Reformation was responsible; if one is an old-fashioned scientist, one naturally thinks that the scientific movement occurred first and powered all the others; and if one is a Marxist, one certainly thinks that the economic and social changes bear the main responsibility.

One factor which must have great relevance here is the undeniable circumstance that the feudalism of Europe and China were fundamentally different. Europe feudalism was military-aristocratic: the peasantry were governed by the knights in their manors, and they in turn were subject to the barons in their castles, while the king in his palace ruled over all. In time of war he needed the help of the lower ranks in the feudal hierarchy who were bound to rally to him with stated numbers of men-at-arms. How different was the feudalism of China, long very justifiably described as bureaucratic. From the time of the first emperor, Ch'in Shih Huang Ti, onwards (third century BC), the old hereditary feudal houses were gradually attacked and destroyed, while the king or emperor (as he soon became) governed by the aid of an enormous bureaucracy, a civil service unimaginable in extent and degree of organization to the petty kingdoms of Europe. Modern research is showing that the bureaucratic organization of China in its earlier stages strongly helped science to grow; only in its later ones did it forcibly inhibit further growth, and in particular prevented a breakthrough which has occurred in Europe. For example, no other country in the world at the beginning of the eighth century AD could have set up a meridian arc survey stretching from south to north some 2500 miles. Nor could it have mounted an expedition at that time to go and observe the stars of the southern hemisphere to within 20° of the south celestial pole. Nor indeed would it have wanted to.

It may well be that a similar pattern will appear in the future when the history of science, technology and medicine, for all the great classical literary cultures, such as India or Sri Lanka, comes to be written and gathered in. Europe has entered into their inheritance, producing an ecumenical universal science and technology valid for every man and woman on the face of the earth. One can only hope that the shortcomings of the distinctively European traditions in other matters will not debauch the non-European civilizations. For example, the sciences of China and of Islam never dreamed of divorcing science from ethics, but when at the Scientific Revolution the final cause of Aristotle was done away with, and ethics chased out of science, things became very different, and more menacing. This was good in so far as it clarified and discriminated between the great forms of human experience, but very bad and dangerous when it opened the way for evil men to use the great discoveries of modern science and activities disastrous for humanity. Science needs to be lived alongside religion, philosophy, history and esthetic experience; alone it can lead to great harm. All we can do today is to hope and pray that the unbelievably dangerous powers of atomic weapons, which have been put into the hands of human beings by the development of modern science, will remain under control by responsible men, and that maniacs will not release upon mankind powers that could extinguish not only mankind, but all life on earth.

(1122 words)

 **Notes**

> Joseph Needham (9 December 1900—24 March 1995), also known as Li Yuese(李约瑟), was a British scientist, historian and sinologist known for his scientific research and writing on the history of Chinese science. He initiated and edited *Science and Civilisation in China*, published by Cambridge University Press.

Task 1 Questions for Comprehension and Discussion

Directions: Please answer the following questions.

1. What are the two fundamental questions raised by the author at the beginning of the writing?
2. What are the examples given by the author to illustrate that the Chinese have been so far in advance of other civilizations?
3. What was the fundamental difference between the feudalism of Europe and that of China? How did the difference influence the development of science and technology in Europe and China?
4. How do China and Islam treat the relationship between science and ethics?

Task 2 Essay Writing

Directions: Next week you are going to join a seminar on the history of technology in China and you are invited to speak about Joseph Needham's view on this issue. Prepare a draft for your speech in 500 words in Chinese, using examples from the text above.